TELLING GOD'S STORY
A PARENTS' GUIDE TO TEACHING THE BIBLE

PETER ENNS

Olive Branch Books
Charles City, Virginia

This book is to be used in conjunction with the *Telling God's Story* series:

Year One Instructor Text and Teaching Guide	978-1-933339-48-1
Year One Student Guide and Activity Pages	978-1-933339-47-4
Year Two Instructor Text and Teaching Guide	978-1-933339-50-4
Year Two Student Guide and Activity Pages	978-1-933339-51-1
Year Three Instructor Text and Teaching Guide	978-1-933339-75-7
Year Three Student Guide and Activity Pages	978-1-933339-76-4

Publisher's Cataloging-In-Publication Data
(Prepared by The Donohue Group, Inc.)

Enns, Peter, 1961-
   Telling God's story : a parents' guide to teaching the Bible / Peter Enns.

   p. : ill., maps ; cm.

   A separate introductory volume to the curriculum, Telling God's story.
   Includes index.
   ISBN: 978-1-933339-46-7

   1. Bible--Study and teaching. 2. Bible--Children's use. 3. Christian education
of children. I. Title.

BS618 .E56 2010
220/.071   2010936481

Maps on pages 69 and 82 created by Sarah Park

For Sue
Mother, Teacher, Fellow Pilgrim

For Erich, Elizabeth, and Sophie
Still on the journey

TABLE OF CONTENTS

Part Two: Reading the Story For Yourself: The Five Acts of the Bible   57

An introduction to the narrative pattern of the Bible

PREFACE

This book introduces parents and teachers to a new philosophy of teaching the Bible. My intent is to give you an overall vision for what the Bible is (and is not), and what it means to read and understand it. My goal is that this will help you teach the Bible faithfully, powerfully, and with joy to your children.

It has been my experience, as a biblical scholar, seminary professor, and parent of three nearly adult children—whom my wife, Sue, homeschooled for part of their secondary school education—that there is a big gap between what children tend to learn about the Bible in the early years, and how Scripture is studied in later years, as children mature into adults. For this reason, I have felt for many years that a different approach to the Bible is needed.

In this introductory volume to studying the Bible, I propose focusing on what the Bible *as a whole* is about, rather than zeroing in on individual Bible stories or snippets of moral teaching taken out of context. This approach introduces young students to the big picture, encouraging them to understand the entire biblical story—as, I believe, it is intended to be understood.

The goal for this kind of approach is to prepare young Christians to have a vibrant faith in God and trust in Scripture in a world that is changing more quickly than we can describe. The chapters that follow will address these two main issues, and others, in more detail.

Telling God's Story stands on its own, as a proposal for a thoughtful, thorough approach to teaching the Bible. But it also acts as the introductory volume for a fully developed curriculum, complete with scripted lessons, activities, and lesson plans. For more on the *Telling God's Story* curriculum, visit olivebranchbooks.net.

I hope that the pattern laid out here will help you develop a real sense of purpose and excitement at the prospect of teaching your children the Christian faith to which our Scripture bears witness. God's word is meant to be taught by faithful parents (Deuteronomy 6:4–9; Proverbs 1:8; 2 Timothy 1:5). This book is intended to aid in that process.

Pete Enns, PhD
Lansdale, PA

Chapter One

Laws About Mildew and Dragons With Crowns

Why the Bible is such a difficult book to teach

Throughout their teenage years, all three of my children have had issues with keeping their rooms even remotely presentable. (One child in particular comes to mind. You know who you are.)

As any parent of teenagers can attest, the dialogue is predictable: "I can't see the floor." "You need dynamite to get from one end of the room to the other." "How can you *live* in this mess?" "I could torch half the clothes on the floor and you wouldn't even miss them." "You kids today; when *I* was your age. . . ."

This has been going on for years, and it gets us nowhere.

Finally, the child with the particular issue and I decided that the main reason for the mess was that there was no good place for organizing clothes. I suddenly saw a ray of hope. I grabbed my keys, hopped in the car, and bought a closet organizing system (a bit pricey, but in times of crisis money is no object). I had it up in two hours, and now my family is living happily ever after (until the next crisis emerges).

For many parents, the Bible looks a little bit like my child's room. It's a mess. Names, places, events are all over the place, and you hardly know where to start cleaning up. It's such a mess, in fact, that if someone ripped twenty pages out of Leviticus or 1 Chronicles, you might not even notice it was missing. And if your aim is to *teach* the Bible to your children, the mess isn't just confusing. It's stressful.

This book is for parents who want to do a good job with the important but daunting task of teaching the Bible. And just like the airplane oxygen mask that you're supposed to put on yourself first before you put it on your children, this book is first and foremost about you.

Take a step back from the thought of teaching your children and focus on yourself for a moment. This is very important, for how *you* see the Bible will influence your children as much as any curriculum.

Think about your own history of reading Scripture. For example, have you ever tried reading the Bible through from beginning to end (maybe as part of a "Bible in a year" reading program of some sort)?

It is January 1, and you are determined to make a go of it. But it's difficult. You start out with the best of intentions, and things coast along well enough for a while. Genesis is pretty interesting, even though it is fifty chapters long. The Joseph story is nice: sexual intrigue, a little spying.

If you make it through Genesis, you've done well and so you begin with Exodus. This is often easier because nearly everyone has seen Charlton Heston portray Moses for half a century now. The special effects are missing from the biblical version (in fact, a fair amount of the movie is nowhere to be found in the pages of Exodus), but you are familiar with the story line and everything is fine . . . until you get to about chapter 20 and start reading all about laws. The Ten Commandments come first. But after the Ten Commandments, chapters 21–23 are filled with the strangest laws,

THIS IS AN INCREDIBLY ACCURATE PICTURE...

about bulls, property lines, servants—not the kinds of things you build your morning devotions around, and certainly not the kinds of things that make sense in the modern West. And how in the world are you supposed to teach this to ten-year-olds?

Then you come to chapter after chapter about the building of the tabernacle. In fact, Exodus 25–40 is all about the tabernacle, with the exception of the golden calf incident in chapters 32–33, which at least introduces some action to the book.

If by some Herculean feat you make it through Exodus, you have to wade through Leviticus, where you hit a brick wall: chapter after chapter of what to sacrifice and when, plus some very strange topics (like how to get rid of mildew). Obviously, you and the Old Testament Israelites breathe a different air. What should you make of all this? And what, if anything, should you teach to your children?

Succumbing to temptation, you skip over to the Psalms ("just for a break; I'll get back to Leviticus"). They seem so nice and uplifting.

Psalm 1: the righteous prosper, the wicked are punished. So far so good. Psalm 2: God's son (i.e., King David) is on the throne. Not sure what that means, but it sounds like good news.

Then you hit Psalms 3, 4, 5, 6, 7, 8, 9. You don't make it out of the teens before the Psalms all start looking the same. You become discouraged, and maybe flip over to Proverbs, but here too: so many sayings, and they all start looking alike. And thirty-one chapters! By this time, it's probably close to spring, so it makes perfect sense to just skip over to the Gospels and forget the rest of the Old Testament. It's almost Easter anyway.

I don't mean to make light of our struggles to understand the Bible, but this is a very common phenomenon among Christians today. The Old Testament is particularly tough to wade through. And as a result the Old Testament, which makes up about 4/5 of our Bible, is something many of us end up avoiding.

Our difficulties with the Old Testament bleed over into our efforts to understand the New. The New Testament is the climax of a grand story, one that begins in the Old Testament, and it echoes back to the Old Testament many, many times. There are about 265 Old Testament passages cited in the New Testament, and some of those are cited more than once—which means that the Old Testament appears over 350 times in the New. That's a lot. My Thinline NIV New Testament is about 265 pages long—which means that there's an average of about 1 1/3 Old Testament citations on each page of the New Testament.

But that's not all. There is more to it than actual *citations*. The New Testament *alludes* to the Old Testament many times without actually quoting it—over 1,000 times!

Take a step back and think about it. The New Testament authors could hardly open their mouths without the Old Testament gushing out.

Yes, the Bible is a detailed, sometimes difficult to follow and understand book, especially the Old Testament. No reason to deny it or be embarrassed for saying it. The prospect of *teaching* the Bible to *one's own children*, when one feels so untrained and even lost, is intimidating.

This book is an attempt to do for you what the closet organizer in my child's room did for me: give some sense of *order and meaning* to the chaos. Rather than avoiding the Bible (as I did that horrible, messy room), you will find Scripture becoming a welcome place. When you're there, you'll feel that you have a handle on what is what, what belongs where, and how to help your children "keep it clean."

The plan I'll lay out in this book is not perfect. It will not take care of every bit of mess and solve every dilemma. But it will help you get a handle on the Bible and its message. (And my child's floor is not spotlessly clean—there are socks here and there, an occasional pile of clothes or candy wrappers—but it is A LOT better.)

• • •

The goal of this approach is not simply for you or your children to understand the Bible. Any teaching of Scripture to children must have a much more practical and deeper purpose: to encourage children to become mature, knowledgeable, and humble followers of Jesus, growing in faith.

Growing in faith is not a contest or part of a daily to-do list. It is a *journey* that *all* Christians are on. Your children have the privilege of beginning that journey under your care and love. Yes, that is a serious responsibility for parents (hence, the anxiety involved). But it is also a *joy* and a *calling* that can be heard echoing through the pages of Scripture. As far back as Exodus, when Moses is giving the instructions for the celebration of Passover, he adds "And when your children ask you 'What does this ceremony mean *to you?*' then tell them. . . ." (Exodus 12:26).

There are two things worth pointing out here. First, children will ask what the ceremony—and, by implication, the teachings of the Scriptures—mean. Second, they will ask what they mean *to you*. Even if they do not ask us in words, they are watching us. So, as parents (and teachers), we must first understand what the Bible means *to us*.

So what is the Bible, and what are we supposed to be doing with it?

These may strike some as two odd questions. After all, the Bible is the Word of God and we are supposed to read it and obey it. Fair enough, but that does not even begin to address the question of what the Bible is *doing*. Why does the Word of God say the things it says? Why does it look the way it looks? And is obedience really the essence of what we are supposed to get out of it?

Of course, the answer is *yes*—in part. But the Bible aims much higher; it teaches us to see ourselves and the world around us in fresh, exciting, and challenging ways. The Bible is not a Christian owner's manual. It bears witness to who God is, what he has done, and who we, as his people, are.

God does not change, and the Gospel bears eternal witness to his unending love for us. Likewise, the core questions of the human drama are now as they have been since the beginning of recorded time: Who are we? Why are we here? What gives meaning to our lives? Does God exist? The Gospel claims to give answers to these types of questions. But the world around us seems to change almost daily. The information our children have access to, as well as the very structure of their lives, has been affected by the rapid shifts in the world around us. As a result, our children ask different questions than children of other generations, and are not as easily satisfied with traditional answers.

Because of this, many parents approach the study and teaching of the Bible with a certain amount of fear: "Can I actually *do this*? What if I make a mistake and ruin my child spiritually? How can I allow children to ask hard questions without them turning out to be heretics?"

Part of the answer is to remember that you are *not* really up for the task—at least not alone. Remember that your children are God's children. It is your calling and responsibility to raise them in a godly way, but don't think for one minute that *their* success rests on *your* skills and abilities. Your children are, after all, God's work in the end. Like all of us, they are embarking on their own spiritual journey.

Furthermore, no Christian is an island. We all must depend on the larger Christian community, the church, to be part of raising our children. (This is normally part of the vow a congregation takes when a child is either baptized or dedicated.) So, have no fear, parents. You *will* make mistakes (although I hope this book will help you make fewer), but remember God's grace is bigger than the best of your intentions. He really loves your children. Look on this not as a worrisome task but as a few precious, golden years of opportunity.

One of the most significant challenges Christian parents face is how to pass on our faith to our children, whom we love deeply and who have been entrusted by the Lord to our care. No curriculum or method will give you the magic key, the simple answer that will make this task easy. But I hope that what is laid out in the pages to follow will aid you and your children on your Christian pilgrimage, so that together you will have a mature and viable Christian faith as you pass through the peaks and valleys of life.

PART ONE

How to Teach the Bible

— Chapter Two —

What the Bible Actually Is (and Isn't)

A clear explanation of the Bible's nature: a complex and fascinating narrative with a beginning, middle, and end—not a book of rules or a manual of morals

What is the Bible? And how does knowing something about what the Bible *is* change the way we read it? When we sit down in the morning, cup of coffee in our hands, ready to give the Bible a good 15–30 minutes, what is it we are supposed to be "doing"? What is supposed to "happen"? What does it mean to read the Bible? What is the Bible there for?

These may seem like odd questions, and too often we don't think to ask them. But we should begin our task of teaching the Bible by becoming more reflective: considering more carefully what the Bible *is*.

It's All about Expectations

The first thing to keep in mind when we read the Bible is the hardest: Don't go straight to the question "What does this mean to me?"

We are constantly told that the Bible is to be applied to our lives, and so we read it looking for ways to make it so. That can lead us to do one of two things: either skip parts that don't apply very easily (the tabernacle section in Exodus) or dig a certain type of application out of each Scripture reading—one that focuses on a concrete behavior that is supposed to stem from that morning's meditation.

I am all for applying the Bible. Don't get me wrong. But a better understanding of the Bible will lead us in another direction. The first question we should ask about what we are reading is not "How does this apply to me?" Rather, it is "What is this passage saying in the context of the book I am reading, and how would it have been heard in the ancient world?"

A good, thorough study Bible will make answering these questions easier. In addition, there are numerous basic "Bible background" kinds of books on the market that are geared toward everyday readers.[1] You don't have to go wild, and you certainly don't have to be an expert! I am only talking about a reorientation; a commitment to learn, slowly but surely, over the years, to ask questions that the *text* is raising. Our first struggle in reading the Bible is to move from the "What about me?" perspective to the "What does this tell us about God in that context?" question.

Knowing something about what the Bible is designed to do, what its purpose is, will help us adjust our expectations about what it is we hope to find in the Bible. If our expectations are

---

[1]Some richly illustrated volumes are John H. Walton and Andrew E. Hill, *Old Testament Today*, and Gary M. Burge, Lynn H. Cohick, and Gene L. Green, *The New Testament in Antiquity* (both published by Zondervan); and Bill T. Arnold and Bryan E. Beyer, *Encountering the Old Testament*, and Walter A. Elwell and Robert W. Yarbrough, *Encountering the New Testament* (both published by Baker).

modern instead of ancient, we will get ourselves into a bind. Before we can ask the hard questions—for example, "Is Genesis 1 in harmony with scientific thought? Or does Genesis 1 trump scientific thought?"—we must ask a more foundational question: *What do we have the right to expect from God's word as a book written in an ancient world?*

Jesus and the Bible Are Similar

Let me give you a challenge that will help you examine your expectations about the Bible: Think of the Bible the way we think of Jesus.

Christianity teaches that Jesus is, mysteriously, both God and human. He is not half one, half the other. He does not appear to be one while "really" being the other. He is both: all God and all human all the time.

Now think of the Bible by drawing a parallel: In the same way that Jesus is both completely divine and human, the Bible also has divine and human dimensions.

Remember, this is only an *analogy*; it certainly does not tell us everything we need to know about the nature of Scripture. But it is a helpful one. Jesus was fully divine and fully human; the Bible is ultimately from God, but every last word of it was written by human beings in certain places and historical settings. Jesus is without sin; and in the same way, the Bible does not fall short of God's purpose.   *I QUITE LIKE THIS PHRASING!*

Think of Jesus, walking around Palestine in the first century. Although he was God's son, there was nothing particularly striking about him. He was easily mistaken for just another Galilean Jew—which is one reason why some people were so amazed at his teaching and miracles, while others were so offended ("Who does this guy think he is?"). In fact, for the most part everything about him said "human." He was born, he had skin and bones, he ate, he laughed, he cried, he wore a robe, he had a Middle Eastern complexion, he wore sandals.

I could go on. My point is that *none of the humanness of Jesus of Nazareth detracts from his being the Son of God.* In fact, through such a lowly state God *chose* to communicate himself. But as human as Jesus was, he was without sin.

Now apply this same point of view to the Bible. If you make a commitment to become more knowledgeable about the ancient world, you will come away realizing how very much at home the Bible was in ancient times. Just like Jesus' clothing and customs were at home in his world, the Bible was written in ancient, very common, languages. It used many of the same expressions and ideas of the ancient world. But because these writings are ultimately from God, they don't "slip up" anywhere. There is no place in the Bible where the Holy Spirit says, "Oops, I really didn't mean to put it that way. Can I have another go at it?" The Bible does exactly what God wants it to do.

Maybe the chart below can help clarify this analogy between Jesus and the Bible.

Jesus	Bible
Both divine and human nature	Both divine and human authorship
Did not sin	Does not misrepresent God
Appeared like an everyday Jew	Appears like an ancient book
Power and authority derived from God	Power and authority derived from God

Jesus was without sin, although fully human. The Bible does not fall short of God's purpose, even though it was written by humans. Both derive their authority by being from God.

Now think carefully about the implications of this.

Considering that Jesus is the Son of God, the Gospels tell us many unexpected things about him. For example, Jesus himself admitted he had limited knowledge. In Matthew 24:36, he says,

"No one knows the day nor the hour, not the angels . . . nor the Son, but only the Father." Luke 2:52 says, "And [the child] Jesus grew in wisdom, and in stature, and in favor with God and men"— meaning that the child Jesus learned things as he went along, like any child does, rather than coming into the world filled with complete divine knowledge. And Jesus died. God is not supposed to die.

The Bible is similar. There are many things about it that we would not expect from a book called "God's Word." Genesis 1 has strong resemblances to other ancient creation stories. Israel has prophets, priests, and kings, all of whom at times look very similar to the prophets, priests, and kings of the other nations in the ancient world. Laws govern the details of daily lives that are very different from our own—and some parts of which have disappeared forever. New Testament Greek is a very simple, common, everyday version of the higher, more polished classical Greek. It is the language of the common people.

But none of these properties of the Bible I just mentioned are examples of the Bible somehow "falling short." Instead they display the humanness of the Bible. They correspond to Jesus' humanity; they are not "errors" that would correspond to Jesus' sin.

If Genesis 1 were to say, for example, that the God of Israel did not make the world, that would be an error. That would be like Jesus cursing the Father; that would be sin. But the fact that Genesis 1 reflects ancient creation stories does not point to error in the Bible, any more than Jesus' wearing sandals and speaking Aramaic was sin.

I hope it is clear what I am after here. Don't expect Jesus to be something he isn't: a king dressed in fine robes, with servants and armies. He was lowly. He came to serve. Likewise, don't expect something from the Bible it can't deliver. Don't expect it to be high and lofty, detached from the ancient world in which it was written.

C. S. Lewis has a great way of putting it. In 1947, J. B. Phillips published a very earthy English translation of the New Testament letters. (You may have heard of Phillips' translation of the entire

New Testament, *The New Testament in Modern English*.) Lewis wrote the introduction, defending Phillips' approach to translating the New Testament in a way that the common people of his day would connect with.

Lewis points out that the Greek style of the New Testament shows that the biblical writers did not have a high command of the language. He defends his point by drawing the same analogy we draw here, between Jesus and the Bible.

> Does this [the low style of NT Greek] shock us? It ought not to, except as the Incarnation itself ought to shock us. The same divine humility which decreed that God should become a baby at a peasant-woman's breast, and later an arrested field-preacher in the hands of the Roman police, decreed also that He should be preached in a vulgar, prosaic and unliterary language. If you can stomach the one, you can stomach the other. The Incarnation is in that sense an irreverent doctrine: Christianity, in that sense, an incurably irreverent religion. When we expect that it should have come before the World in all the beauty that we now feel in the Authorized [King James] Version we are as wide of the mark as the Jews were in expecting that the Messiah would come as a great earthly King. The real sanctity, the real beauty and sublimity of the New Testament (as of Christ's life) are of a different sort: miles deeper or *further in*.[2]

No one says it like C. S. Lewis: Allow the Bible to be the Bible.

Neither Jesus nor the Bible are quite what we might have expected. And it is precisely *that fact* that drives us to see a more real beauty and sublimity in *both*. Sometimes we know the Bible too well; it becomes tame and predictable. But if we look at the Bible as ancient people would have read it, we can be as struck as they were by the power and authority of its message.

---

[2]C. S. Lewis, "Introduction" to J. B. Phillips, *Letters to Young Churches: A Translation of the New Testament Epistles* (London: Geoffrey Bles, 1947), vii–viii.

The Bible Is Not a Rule Book or an Owner's Manual; It Takes Wisdom

If we take seriously the likeness between Christ and the Bible, we will discover that one of the most common ways of looking at the Bible soon becomes very inadequate.

I remember, in my early twenties, reading a book of advice from a pastor who answered questions that people wrote in to him. Many of these people were looking to orient their lives around the Bible; they were looking to the Bible for answers to life's questions.

Few Christians would find fault with this, but consider the following. One woman asked whether, biblically speaking, it was acceptable for Christians to go to the circus. The pastor answered that there was no clear biblical passage that addressed this issue. But then he proceeded to bring together a number of passages from various parts of the Bible and use them to prove his conclusion: Indeed, biblically speaking, it was *not* a good idea to go to the circus.

I laughed good and long when I read this. But since then, my wife and I have done our best to raise three children. Now I realize that parents do indeed crave these sorts of answers to everyday questions about behavior and cultural norms; and they feel, because the Bible is God's word, it should *give* those answers to everyday questions.

The problem is that the Bible is not that kind of book. We need to learn the kinds of issues the Bible addresses so we can *learn to ask the questions of the Bible that the Bible is meant to answer.* The Bible is not a book on how to invest your money, which political party to join, whether to homeschool, where to go to college, whom to marry, where to live, whether you should buy that car, America as God's chosen people, or a blueprint for present-day world events. It is not, in other words, a "Christian owner's manual." Too many Christians assume that the Bible is the guidebook to address all of life's questions. But that is not what the Bible is designed to do.

The Bible tells the story of how God's people are delivered from death to life, and as a result are now called upon to live a life in harmony with that high calling (this occupies much of Paul's letters). The New Testament in particular describes all sorts of situations faced by early Christians, and the New Testament writers guide these first Christians through each issue. For us today, when we read the New Testament, what we see is a *portrait being painted for us of what a life in Christ looks like.* We are being given the vision of what a Christian life looks like.

What is *not* addressed in the Bible are specifically modern situations. There is no Bible verse that will, either directly or indirectly, answer many of the questions that confront Christian families today: When do you begin dating? Is it OK to watch an R-rated movie? What kinds of books should your children read? What sort of education should they receive?

In this light, I want to introduce what I think is the single most important biblical concept for living a Christian life, not only today, but during any era: wisdom.

Let me give an example.

When my son was twelve, he asked if we could watch the R-rated movie *Saving Private Ryan* together. "All" of his friends had already seen it, and he didn't want to be the oddball.

Ultimately, we watched the movie together. But before we did, I had to consider a number of factors. What was his personality type? What kind of internal "filters" did he have? Was this the right time and place to put him in a controlled setting that might help him grow?

In our particular situation, watching that movie was a tremendously positive experience for him. (The opening battle scene was the most graphic representation of war he had ever seen, and it helped him understand how horrible war is.) Some might think that the violence and dialogue in the movie are inappropriate for a twelve-year-old. I certainly understand the point, but quoting Proverbs 22:6, as one shocked parent did, is not going to resolve the issue: "Train a child in the way he should go, and when he is old he will not turn from it."

The truth is that this famous proverb is often misunderstood. It doesn't mean "How you train your child will determine his or her life path," as if a parent's patient, daily influence will guarantee results, while if you make mistakes the child will stumble. Instead, it means that a commitment to train your children in wisdom will bear fruit when they come of age, but there are no guarantees.

However one understands the proverb, it takes wisdom to know how *that* proverb applies to *this* situation—which means understanding the proverb, having an intimate knowledge of the circumstances, and then using both to make a decision. In my opinion, I *did* apply the wisdom of Proverbs 22:6 by allowing my son to watch an R movie (even if others disagree).

Now maybe that one example is enough to make you want to throw this book into the fireplace. I hope not. When we get down to it, much of our lives as Christians requires us, as a wise friend once said to me, to "wing it." I don't mean that the Christian life is haphazard with no guidance. I mean that many of the decisions we are called upon to make every day we make, not because of a verse here or there, but because of the wisdom we have accumulated over the years. That wisdom is acquired through the study of Scripture, prayer, life in a Christian community (not just "going to church"), and plain old life experiences (otherwise known as learning from your mistakes).

I am a wiser man today in my late forties than I was at thirty-five or twenty-five, not because I am, all of a sudden, a better Bible reader, but because a lot of things have happened to me through the years. And I am thankful that I have been supported, as I've dealt with the ins and outs of life, by a lot of wise people. I am responsible for passing that wisdom on to my children, both in word and in deed (and we all know the latter is much harder).

Our lives are a journey, and raising our children is part of that journey. We are in a constant search to conform our lives to the patterns that are modeled for us in the Bible and in Christian community. When we look to the Bible to see those patterns, we read it differently than if we were treating the Bible as an owner's manual. Looking to the Bible in this way requires a sober and mature recognition that the Bible is, in some ways, much more *restricted* in its scope than we sometimes assume. (It will certainly not tell you whether or not to go to the circus.)

However, if we learn to hear what the Spirit is saying through these ancient yet transcendent writings, we will see that the Bible is much *more* than we bargained for. The Bible is not a book primarily devoted to *what we should do*. Instead, it is devoted to telling us *who we are* and how our behaviors should reflect that reality.

This allows the Bible to affect us on a much deeper level than if we think of it as a book of scattered rules that only the most diligent can find and follow. The Bible is a deeply vision-setting book that gives us a powerful look at what life in Christ can be. This perspective may not be as easy or comfortable as thinking of the Bible as a rulebook to follow, but it is much longer lasting!

Why am I making such a big point out of all this? Because if you can give your children this vision of the Gospel message, it will grow with them as they grow and gain independence in this world. If the Bible is primarily a book of morals and principles, it becomes much smaller—and much less applicable to the situations in which they will find themselves as their lives become progressively more complicated.

The story the Bible tells, which culminates in the Gospel, both disorients and reorients us. The Bible does not tell us about a religion that we practice; it points us to rebirth, a transformation, a whole new way of being. This, I think, has been lost on our young people; and when the vision is lost, they wind up abandoning their faith, blaming it for failing to "connect" with their world.

But if their faith does not connect to their world, it was misrepresented—mistaught—to them in the first place.

With this in mind we move now to a proposal for teaching the Bible to our young people in a way that brings out the full complexity and power of the Bible's vision. Rather than beginning with Genesis, as so many programs do, we will begin with Jesus, the author and perfecter of our faith (Hebrews 12:2).

Chapter Three

Teaching the Bible as God's Story

The three stages of teaching the Bible: elementary, middle grades, and high school

The Elementary Years: Knowing Jesus— Who He Was, What He Did, What He Said

As we teach the youngest children—those in grades one through four—the primary emphasis should be on Jesus. This makes the approach I'll outline here different from most other Bible curricula.

Don't get me wrong. All Christian educational materials get to Jesus sooner or later. But I propose getting to him right at the outset.

It seems to me that the overriding emphasis in the Christian education of our children is to get them to know the *Bible*. This tends to make early-grade materials heavy on character studies

WHILE THE BIBLE ITSELF WANTS TO ~~GET~~ HELP US KNOW JESUS...

(learning about the life of David), individual stories (the Creation, the Flood), or moral lessons (what we should learn about life as a Christian from the example of Daniel in the lion's den).

I am not saying that listening to Bible stories and learning about important biblical characters is wrong, nor that deriving proper patterns of behavior from the Bible is off-limits. But it is vitally important that children have the proper foundation underneath their faith from the very beginning.

The proper foundation is now what it has been since the first Christmas: Jesus.

Jesus is the focal point of the Christian Bible. This doesn't mean that we have to "find Jesus" in every verse of the Old Testament. Rather, the Bible as a whole is going somewhere, and that "somewhere" is actually a "someone."

The Bible does not exist to talk about itself. It exists to reveal who God is, what he has done, and who we are as a result. The absolute center of all this is Jesus, who he was, what he did, and what he said—or as theologians sometimes put it, "the person and work of Christ."

Of course, knowing something about the content of the Bible as a whole will help you understand better how Jesus is its goal and center. That might suggest that a book-by-book ("start with Genesis 1") approach would supply the best foundation for learning about Jesus.

Let me suggest an alternative plan.

In the early church, after Jesus' ascension, the Gospel was being preached to Jew and Gentile alike. Some Jews had a strong background in their own story (the Old Testament writings), but for Gentiles all this was new. When the apostles began to proclaim Christ, they did not first hold a sixteen-week study on the Old Testament and then announce, "OK, *now* we're ready to talk about Jesus."

Rather, in the early church, Jesus was proclaimed to the Jews as their messiah (see Chapter 8, which will tell you exactly what "messiah" meant to the Jews), and to the Gentiles as their Lord, a term that had definite political overtones at the time (*Caesar* claimed to be the "lord" of the people). That proclamation was accompanied by all sorts of miracles: Pentecost, raising the dead, healings. The proclamation was also demonstrated, very visibly, by the qualities of character that appeared in Jesus' earliest followers: joyful willingness to suffer and die for Jesus' sake and for the further spread of the Gospel; self-sacrifice for others; generosity; forgiveness; and much more.

In other words, the apostles didn't start with the background stuff. They got right to the point and talked about Jesus.

Yes, we're talking about teaching children here, and the Gospel was spread in the early church through adults. But the same principle remains important. *The point of Scripture is ultimately to introduce people to Jesus.* He is what makes the Christian faith unique; not moral teaching, not Bible stories, but a man who was also God, who did and said amazing and challenging things, and who was dead but is no longer so. We hope for our children to know this Jesus—not to develop an encyclopedic knowledge of the Bible.

Knowing Scripture is important. But knowledge of Scripture does not necessarily lead to knowledge of Christ. The two are not to be divorced, but neither are they to be equated. I think everyone reading this knows people who have relatively limited or "lay" knowledge of the Bible and are vibrant and mature Christians. And I know too many people whose knowledge of Scripture can make most people squirm, but whom I wouldn't allow to feed my children, let alone teach them. (I'm exaggerating a bit, but not much.)

By beginning in the earliest years of teaching with a focus on Jesus, you focus first on the point of the whole biblical story. You demonstrate to your children the ultimate payoff for knowing their Bibles: knowing Jesus. In the next few years, grades five through eight—a time when young students begin to think much more critically and are able to grapple with more complexity—you will spend much more time on teaching them the flow of the biblical story as a whole.

An analogy might help. From the time your children are very young, you begin teaching them the importance of respecting you as their parents. This begins very simply: say please, no whining, no hitting, no falling on the floor and screaming. As they get older, your children take this framework of respect and use it to deal with new situations. They do not forget (we hope!) the former lesson ("respect your parents"), but now this simple lesson is fleshed out to address new situations: "Do not speak to me in a disrespectful tone of voice"; "Do not manipulate me by telling a half truth"; "Respecting your parents includes respecting other adults who care for you"; and so on.

If we can give our children a firm, age-appropriate grasp of Jesus and his ministry—where he came from, why he came, what he taught, where he went, where he is now—we will build for them a good foundation. This will allow them to begin to know him in a much more complex way as they move into the middle-school and high-school years and begin to understand the other parts of the story—the ones that flesh out the larger purpose of Jesus' ministry, his bringing of the kingdom of God.

An important dimension of this approach is a focus on the love Jesus has for children. Most Christian parents know the saying found in Matthew, Mark, and Luke: "Let the little children come to me, and do not hinder them, for the kingdom of God belongs to such as these." Jesus does not *want* his disciples trying to keep these annoying kids out of the messiah's way, and his response should warm every parent's heart.

Although I don't want to hang an entire Bible study method on this single verse, I do see in this story a general principle for teaching our children. We should not "hinder" children by placing obstacles in their path that they may not yet be prepared to understand. Let me speak plainly: children should be introduced to Jesus without parents feeling the pressure of downloading every important piece of biblical teaching into their young minds at the same time.

Let me explain.

Jesus is described in full color in the Gospels. He weeps, laughs, becomes angry, has compassion, loves, has determination, prefers times of isolation, grows tired. In the early grades, we should focus on bringing out this full portrait of Jesus. What should *not* be emphasized is the child's miserable state of sin and the need for a savior.

Please do not misunderstand me. I believe Jesus rescues us from our sin. But we cannot and should not expect adult comprehension of the depth of sin and the grace of God from our children. As parents, we can be so concerned that our very young children make a "profession of faith" that, without wanting in any way to harm the child, we wind up manipulating the child rather than teaching. The child knows that we want him to be baptized, or confirmed, or dedicated; and if the child loves you, he will do his best to comply.

But we must remember that *our children's salvation is not our work, it is the work of the Spirit.*

Fuller lessons concerning sin and grace will come in time, and certainly parents and churches have the responsibility to teach the fullness of what the Bible has to offer. But most young children simply do not have the emotional or intellectual maturity to grasp the *adult* concepts in the Bible. Children need to be approached as *children*, and Jesus approached children by blessing them, praying for them, and reassuring them of his love for them. There will be plenty of time as your child begins to mature to discuss the biblical story as a whole and lay out the entire dysfunctional human drama—at a time when your child can begin to grasp its implications.

Do not allow yourself to be convinced that you are somehow shortchanging your children by not addressing adult concepts at such a young age. By teaching them about the life and message of Jesus, you are actually building a foundation that will allow the broader biblical story to be better understood; you are laying the base of a road that the child will travel down during an entire lifetime of Christian pilgrimage.

I believe in God's displeasure with sin. But to introduce children to the God of wrath right at the beginning of their lives, without the requisite biblical foundation and before the years of emotional maturity, can actually *distort* their view of God. What children do understand is warmth, comfort, acceptance: "Little children, *come to me!*"

Having said all this, let me add that you can't talk about Jesus for too long without seeing him get upset with people—mostly the self-confident religious elite. He becomes angry, speaks some harsh words, and is even sarcastic at times. We will certainly take this head on, but the fully realized Jesus of the Gospels is intended for adult consumption.

To put the Gospels within reach of children, we should begin by teaching them, in very concrete terms, about the numerous acts of mercy and compassion that Jesus performed—especially for those who were down and out. Weary, sinful, desperate people who lived in his day and knew nothing of the ultimate significance of his coming nevertheless were drawn to him. Jesus spoke and acted in a "powerfully gentle" way. We should focus, early on, on these types of episodes: Luke 9:10–17; Matthew 8:5–13; Matthew 19:13–15; Matthew 11:28–30.

We should also teach our children about the major episodes of Jesus' life: his birth, his years of ministry, the Passion Week, his resurrection and ascension. The difficulty here is that some of this can be pretty abstract for young children, not to mention upsetting. (I remember being a bit freaked out by the crucifixion when I was six or seven.)

Again, age-appropriateness is key. You can introduce young children to the central principles of the Passion Week without feeling that you need to fill in every single detail. For example, you can say, "Jesus loves you so much he died for you," without examining the exact nature of crucifixion. There will be time for that in subsequent years.

We should also be concerned with showing our children what it means to be a follower of Jesus. In the New Testament, "I will follow" is more or less equivalent to "I believe." There is no mere intellectual belief in the New Testament; the whole *person* follows

Jesus. So we should examine not only the life of Jesus, but the actions of his disciples—and the challenges Jesus issues to them as he calls them to follow.

So during grades one through four, you should focus on the same thing that the Bible as a whole focuses on: Jesus, the parables he told, his miracles, his teachings, his life, his disciples, and the culmination of his life.

The Middle-Grade Years: Getting a Big Picture of the Bible

In many ways, these grades are the most important of all. Your aim in grades five through eight—the middle-school years—should be to take the Jesus that your children have already been introduced to, and place him into the larger context of Scripture as a whole.

This may seem backwards, but *knowing where the story ends up* will help you put the earlier pieces of the story more firmly into place. Think of a novel or movie you like. You've read (or watched) it more than once, even though you know the end—because knowing the ending helps you appreciate more deeply the events that lead up to that end.

When children look at Jesus first, they are able to begin thinking of Scripture as a *coherent story*, not a random assembly of Bible stories. They begin to learn here that the Bible is essentially a "narrative" (although it is not necessary to use that word).

To go back to the analogy I used at the very beginning of this book, beginning with Jesus is the best way I know of bringing some organization to the room. Or, better yet, think of Jesus as the closet! He is the grand organizing "space" within which we, as Christians, understand all of the Bible. In the middle grades, children will begin to gain a certain number of very important, heavy-duty hooks to hang in this closet.

In other words, now is the time to look at the grand narrative, the Bible as a whole, and to examine the individual acts in the story that together make up this enormous biblical narrative. In

Part Two, I will lay out both the individual acts and the overall pattern for you, so that you can help your children begin to see how each of these acts support the overall focus of the Bible on the person and work of Jesus.

Let me be very clear about one thing here. When you read, say, the story of David, you should not approach it by saying, "Hey, David is just like Jesus!" Looking toward Jesus as the culmination of the story does not mean that you should "jump to Jesus" every few seconds while ignoring the shape and reality of the Old Testament stories themselves.

Instead, the better that middle-grade students come to know the stories and patterns of the Old Testament, the better they will begin to see the dramatic and sometimes unexpected ways in which Jesus brought final expression to the Old Testament. As we teach our middle-grade students, we should try to avoid two extremes: focusing so much on Jesus that the wonderful twists and turns, peaks and valleys, of the Old Testament story itself are obscured— and focusing so much on the Old Testament *as an end in itself* that the ultimate message of Scripture, Jesus (which the New Testament authors are so intent to proclaim), gets lost.

Speaking more concretely: in the middle grades, children should learn the basic flow of the biblical story. They should learn the basic timeline of Israel's history. Its beginnings were small: one family, the children of Abraham, Israel's first ancestor, and his wife Sarah. This family line continued through Isaac (and Rebekah), Jacob (and Rachel), and then Jacob's twelve sons, who made up the tribes of Israel. Jacob's son Joseph was sold into Egyptian slavery only to rise to second in command under Pharaoh.

All this occurred in the first half of the second millennium B.C., according to the biblical timeline. This set the stage for the next part of Israel's journey: its tribal existence. Middle-grade students should know that the Israelites were first welcomed to Egypt under Joseph, only to be enslaved several generations later. Moses arose, chosen by God, to deliver the Israelites from bondage and bring them to Mount Sinai. There they received the Law and instructions for building the tabernacle, God's portable center of worship. After forty years of wandering in the wilderness, the Israelites crossed into the Promised Land under Joshua's leadership and began a lengthy period of conquest of the cities of Canaan, which marked the outset of international strife that would mark Israel's entire history.

These events took up the second half of the second millennium B.C. and prepared the way for the period of Israel's monarchy. Children should know about the three kings who ruled all of Israel in succession: Saul, David, and David's son Solomon. Both David and Solomon stood as models of kingship for generations, despite their personal shortcomings.

Next, young students should learn about the fragmentation of Israel. After Solomon, Israel divided into two kingdoms: the north and south. The northern kingdom lasted only about 200 years until it fell to the mighty Assyrians, never to be heard from again. The southern nation also met its demise, although it lasted another 140 years before falling to the new superpower of the time, Babylon. The southern kingdom, also known as the kingdom of Judah, went into exile for about fifty years.

These events took place in the first half of the first millennium B.C. and bring us to the end of Israel's continuous possession of its own land. After returning from exile, the Israelites nevertheless were subject to a succession of superpowers who controlled their land: first the Persians, then the Greeks, and finally the Romans.

This brings us to the time of Jesus.

When students of the Bible learn to control this basic outline of Israel's history, many important hooks and hangers will be added to their closet organizers. They should also begin to get a feel for the different genres—or literary styles—of the Bible. Although much of the Old Testament is written in a narrative style, there is also prophetic literature, much of which is written in a poetic style that takes some getting used to. Other poetic books such as Psalms, Proverbs, and Job pose their own challenges in understanding. It is important for students to begin to see that we cannot expect the same kinds of things from, say, a historical narrative like 1 Kings and a poetic wisdom book like Ecclesiastes. What do prophecy, historical writing, or poetry look like?

Realize that you still do not need to go through every book of the Bible in excruciating detail. (I think every parent of middle-schoolers can give a hearty amen to that). The middle-grade years are the "hook and hanger stage," providing students with the most important "pegs" in the biblical story on which to hang more detailed knowledge as they grow. It is less important that the children know who Bezalel and Oholiab are (see Exodus 31) than to understand how the Exodus and the tabernacle fit into the overall biblical story. Children who learn the story of David and Goliath should also grasp what a king like David represented for Israel, and how a figure like David fits into the grand biblical narrative.

Despite my strictures about not reading the Bible as an "owner's manual," it will be important for you to also encourage your students to look for connections between the biblical story and their own lives. This isn't always going to be easy, and there's nothing more tedious than forcing a moral lesson from a section of Scripture where, frankly, there really isn't one (e.g., try applying the plague of gnats to your life). But at any point in the biblical story we can learn something about who God is and what he is doing. Just remember that the individual parts of the story are, in the end, subsumed under the authority of the risen Christ, about whom Scripture ultimately speaks.

Grades 9–12: Understanding the Bible in Its Settings

Teenagers have their finger on the pulse of our culture in ways we do not. I have been painfully reminded of this on a regular basis—from trying to get my teens to listen to 70s rock, to assuming that pot is hard to come by and that only the rare teen is sexually active.

During these years, your task should be to prepare students to understand the Bible in a way that allows them to live in and interact with the world around us. In order to do this, the teen-ager needs to begin interacting with the Bible in its historical context.

Now, on one level, pretty much every Christian does this already. All you have to do is open up the NIV Study Bible, with its footnotes, charts, maps, and so on, to see that understanding the historical setting of biblical books will help you understand the Bible better.

But the historical context of Scripture can sometimes challenge our faith as well. Read *Time* or *Newsweek*, or watch the History Channel or PBS around the major holidays, and you'll see that biblical history is considered newsworthy. The focus may be on some recent "evidence" uncovered to tell us what "really" happened to Jesus, or on a newly recovered "lost gospel" that helps us see the "real" Jesus (this kind of thinking underlies Dan Brown's block-buster *The Da Vinci Code*).

Seeing and hearing this sort of thing, as the secular world grap-ples with the historical background of the Bible, is unavoidable for Christian families, and we should not try to insulate ourselves. In previous decades, it might have been possible to live your whole life without ever pondering some of these issues, but chances are our children will not be able to do so. Interest in the Bible, most often coming from a position of skepticism (as well as ignorance—see, again, *The Da Vinci Code*), is all around them. They need to under-stand the issues involved.

Understanding the historical context in which the Bible was written will certainly give them a more informed faith. But even more importantly, understanding how the Bible fits into its setting will help them to see more clearly the kind of God we have.

Let me draw this out a bit more. Studying the world in which the Bible was written can help us understand the Bible better, but it also presents a challenge. For example, it can be unsettling to learn that Genesis 1 has elements in common with creation stories of the ancient world—and that those creation stories are older than the Bible. The same goes for the Flood story.

The Bible seems to fit quite well in this ancient world—perhaps a little too well. As we study, the Bible can begin to look less unique: less like God's word.

Unfortunately, Christians are often first exposed to the cultural contexts of the Bible in hostile—or at least spiritually insensitive—settings. All parents have heard cautionary tales about high-school and college students who take a "Bible as Literature" or "Introduction to the Bible" course and come away confused and unsettled. Some lose their faith.

In those classes they learn that the Genesis story of creation is one that bears striking similarities to other ancient stories. They see that Israel's laws look very similar to other ancient law codes, most of them older than Moses. They see that portions of Job and Proverbs are similar to the wisdom literature of Mesopotamian and Egyptian texts. And more.

They may be shaken to see how similar the Bible is to ancient literature in general. And then they conclude that, since the Bible is so similar to other ancient texts, it is really nothing all that special or different. In fact, this very point of view is often suggested by the teachers and professors themselves (some with very innocent motives, some who are more bitter). Young Christians can easily leave a setting like this with the following logical stream of thought: "If the Bible is so much like other ancient texts, and if these other ancient texts are just not true, well . . . maybe the Bible isn't true either" (or as a professor of mine once said, "It's all a pack of lies").

But this conclusion is premature. There are many, many people in the world who know these issues very well—indeed, studying the Bible's contexts is their life's work—but who do not arrive at the same conclusion. There is no need to follow the train of thought that ends: "The Bible is not entirely unique, *therefore* the Bible is not God's word."

Remember our starting point: Jesus and the Bible are similar. In the same way that we would not expect Jesus to be alien in his culture, we should not expect the Bible to be alien in its culture(s). We should challenge the idea that the similarities are a strike against our faith.

How do we begin to do that? By studying how the Bible fits into the cultures that surrounded it during its composition. Far from diminishing the Bible, this will help us come to understand the Bible better. And this in turn will lead us to know God better: the God who, by his wisdom, has given us a Bible that fits so well into the ancient cultures in which it was written.

A Bible that looks too much like other texts from the ancient world is *not* a problem for people who believe the Bible is God's word. There is virtually nothing in the Bible that can't be further clarified, augmented, or fleshed out by understanding something of the ancient world in which the Bible was written. Perhaps most important among these, as I have been hinting, are the opening chapters of Genesis. Generations of discoveries from the ancient Mesopotamian world have shed invaluable light on how these stories are meant to be understood. The same goes for understanding some of what we read in the story of Abraham and the other ancestors. We now know, too, that Israel's laws were not unique, but reflected legal traditions of numerous cultures during and before Israel's time. Israel's wisdom literature also reflects its cultural environment. Little in the Bible has remained untouched by these discoveries, and no student of the Bible can afford to be unaware of their significant impact.

This is true not only of writings but of virtually anything you can think of from Israel's culture. Temples, priests, sacrifices, prophets, kings: none is completely unique to Israel. All have counterparts in other ancient cultures older than Israel.

This is the Bible we have. As we come to understand these things better, we will come to understand better what God is (and was) doing with his people. Study of the Bible's composition and its contexts will not present an obstacle to faith; but it will challenge and deepen faith, even as it nudges us out of our comfort zones.

In my experience, when parents and churches are more intentional in introducing students to the issues that are *routinely* discussed in our contemporary world about the Bible (rather than avoiding or dismissing them), the faith of our young people is strengthened. They develop a more mature understanding of Scripture and the Gospel, and a more mature faith in Christ. They will also be better equipped to think soberly about challenges they *will* encounter in other settings, without feeling that loss of faith is the necessary next step.

— Chapter Four —

Traditional Approaches: Drawbacks and Misunderstandings

How other approaches (the "Bible Story"
approach, the "Character Study" approach,
the "Defending the Bible" approach)
shortchange the Bible and can lead to
misunderstanding

We've described a three-part pattern of study: focus on Jesus in the elementary years, concentration on the larger picture of the entire biblical story during the middle-grade years, and critical examination of the historical contexts surrounding the Bible in high school. I certainly don't mean to imply that your children will be permanently shortchanged if you don't follow this pattern. But this three-part approach *does* differ significantly from traditional approaches of teaching the Bible—and those differences are worth highlighting.

Not a "Bible Story" Approach

The first difference is something I've mentioned already, but it's worth revisiting in a little more detail.

It's very common to teach children "Bible stories" as they begin their Christian education. On some levels this makes perfect sense. Children can easily grasp stories with vivid characters and lots of action: the Flood, Tower of Babel, the Exodus, the walls of Jericho. As they listen to these stories, they become increasingly familiar with the Bible—particularly the Old Testament. And the stories hold their attention.

These are laudable goals, and many people have been brought up on the faith this way. I do not want to give the impression that this is a hopelessly flawed method and has to be cast aside.

But I do want to suggest that the "Bible Story" approach sells the Bible short and may, at the end of the day, obscure some important aspects of the Bible—especially as children grow older. As they move into adulthood, those familiar, often-repeated Bible stories can take on an air of being, well, *children's* stories. After all, our young people have read (and watched on TV) all sorts of *other* stories intended for children. And they've grown out of them. So an obvious question comes to their minds: "Why hold on to those Bible stories that were taught as children's stories (complete with cartoon illustrations!) while leaving behind every other children's story?"

Good question. To answer that the Bible is different because it is God's word doesn't help. It just raises another question: Why is God's word filled with children's stories? And if that's the kind of thing the Bible contains, why should I believe the rest of it?

This hit home to me many years ago when my son was six. I was reading the Bible to him, and I'd chosen Genesis 3, the story of the serpent in the Garden.

As I read, he began to get irritated and impatient with me. I asked what the problem was. He said, "Daddy, animals *can't talk*."

Well, he had a point. I thought of responding "Well, in the Bible they do!" but that might have made matters worse—in the cartoons and picture books he was also reading, animals were talking all over the place. If I'd told him that animals can *really* talk in the Bible, but that when animals talk in other books it's just pretend, I would have reinforced the cognitive dissonance he was already experiencing in his little mind.

I wasn't sure what to say. I think I changed the subject.

The issue here is not whether animals talk in the Bible. The issue is that I read him a *very* complex and intricate biblical narrative—the story of Adam, Eve, and the serpent—as if it were a child's story. This biblical story was meant to convey something profound, mature, and foundational to ancient Israelites. Sitting down and reading this story with my son set him up to receive it as one tall tale among others.

The Garden narrative is deeply theological and symbolic. Despite the neat talking snake, it is not the type of story that we should toss casually to our young children. When, at a more mature age, children are asked to revisit this story and begin dealing with it in earnest, many can hardly refrain from snickering. ("I outgrew talking animals years ago!")

Or consider another Bible story commonly taught to children: the story of the Flood. The boat, the animals, the rain, the drama—all lend themselves to videos, snappy tunes, macaroni art, flannel graphs, and furry friends. What is obscured is the simply horrific notion that God would bring down such drastic destruction on the earth, rather than finding some other solution to humanity's rebellion. And *that* is a question young adults *should ask*. It should not be eclipsed by the childhood memory of giraffes walking up the ark's ramp.

Even more vital for our understanding of the Bible: When we reduce the Flood to a children's story, we lose sight of the connection between the waters that come crashing down upon the earth and those very same waters that God had moved to a safe distance in Genesis 1. Grasping what God does in the Flood and why requires a basic working knowledge of the ancient world, not to mention a basic awareness of the interconnection between this story and various other biblical episodes. All of this is beyond what young children can do.

This is why I suggest beginning instead with stories of Jesus.

Certainly the life of Jesus was also written for adult consumption, and the Gospels tell a nuanced story. The difference is that with Jesus, we are not looking at highly complex narratives that require a lot of intellectual maturity to grasp. The stories of Jesus can be appreciated on various levels without reducing their *truth*— as has been demonstrated by the church for 2,000 years.

One example: the Sermon on the Mount. You'll experience the Sermon on the Mount with some added theological punch if you understand that Jesus is portrayed as the new Moses, on a *mountain* giving a new *law*. (Note how many of Jesus' comments begin "You have heard it said, but I say to you. . . .") This is especially meaningful in Matthew's Gospel, which is directed at a Jewish audience. Matthew is saying to his readers "Jesus is the new and better Moses."

But at the same time, "Blessed are the meek," or "Do not worry," or "Do not judge" can be read and understood with great profit by those who aren't aware of this important theological connection.[3]

It may seem appropriate to educate our children in the Bible by increasing their familiarity with Bible stories, but in the long run this may wind up obscuring the Bible. Or worse, it may make the biblical message appear childish and out of touch at a time in their lives when our children may need the Bible the most. By grounding them in the stories of Jesus, which are foundational to our faith, we are building a vital base for a lifelong study of Scripture.

---

[3]In the complete curriculum that spells out this approach for grades one through four, you will actually find two lessons for each passage. One is geared toward the parents and gives a brief but in-depth look at the passage for adults, and the other is a simplified version for the children.

Not a "Character Study" Approach

Closely related to the "Bible Story" approach is the "Character Study" approach: drawing out life lessons by looking at the lives of important biblical characters.

Once again, I am not suggesting that there is *no* value in looking closely at the moral conduct of biblical figures. In fact, such an approach is not only common among Christians, but has been very common in Judaism, even before the time of Christ. But what I said about the "Bible Story" approach holds here as well: We are selling the Bible short if our first reflex is to do character studies and leave it at that.

For children, of course, one of the advantages of character studies is that they are *concrete*. The characters they read about are real people, modeling real behavior. And models of behavior are an important aspect in our faith. Think of Paul's admonition in 1 Corinthians 4:16, "Therefore I urge you to imitate me."

But is that what these people are *doing* in Scripture? Giving us models of behavior?

I think not.

We need only look at how far short virtually every biblical character falls in achieving moral ideals. There is hardly a central biblical figure whose foibles and failings are not paraded front and center, often with little or no condemnation or even explanation.

Noah was "righteous" and "blameless" (Genesis 6:9), and so was chosen to build the ark. But we are never told just what he did to deserve this honor. What does it mean to be righteous and blameless? What is the standard that is being used? (This question has vexed biblical interpreters since before the time of Christ.) Furthermore, the story of Noah and the Flood is hardly about *Noah's* righteousness, but actually God's. It is about how God looks at humanity's failure to act like those created in his image (Genesis 1:26). To read it as a story that conveys how good Noah was is to miss the central concern of the story.

Abraham is, along with Moses, one of the two central figures in the Old Testament (David comes in at a close but clear third). Abraham is chosen to continue God's redemptive plan. But in Genesis 12, no reason is given for *why* this honor should be bestowed upon Abraham.

Yes, Abraham has his great moments in Genesis. He has the faith to obey God and leave Haran in chapter 12. He comes to Lot's rescue in a military campaign (chapter 14). He courageously pleads for the life of the righteous inhabitants of Sodom and Gomorrah (chapter 18).

But he isn't a model of virtue. We shouldn't minimize his willingness to appease Pharaoh by passing off Sarah as his sister in order to protect his own life. (This is very explicit in 12:12–13). In 15:6 we read that Abraham trusted God to keep his promise to give him many children, but just two verses later he questions whether God will give him the Promised Land. In chapter 16 he doesn't stand in the way as Sarah's jealousy gets the better of her and she mistreats her servant Hagar to the point where she and her infant son Ishmael flee into the desert to certain death.

Later, when God promises Abraham that he and Sarah will bear a child in their old age, Abraham laughs (17:17). Sarah has the same reaction in 18:12. Then in chapter 20, apparently not having learned his lesson the first time, Abraham finds himself in Gerar, willing to pass off Sarah as his sister again. In fact, Abimelech, who knows nothing of God, is simply stunned that Abraham would stoop so low.

In one of the most famous stories in the Bible, Abraham is commanded by God to take his son Isaac up on one of the mountains of Moriah and sacrifice him. Apart from the question of why God would ever even ask such a thing (another story that is far too theologically loaded to address with young children), we see that the purpose of the request was to *test* Abraham. As we read in Genesis 22:12, after Abraham successfully passes the test, God says "Now I know that you fear God." On the one hand, this is certainly a story of one man's faith. But on the other hand, Abraham's faith is apparently one that needed testing. After all, he hasn't been doing all that great up to now.

So Abraham's life is not one story of obedience after another. Rather, it is marked by ups and downs. What we really see in these stories is *God's faithfulness* in sticking with Abraham. This is more God's story than Abraham's. If we focus on Abraham as a model of virtue, we may miss the core of the story's message.

The parade of biblical characters doesn't get much better. Jacob, later renamed Israel, is to become the father of the twelve tribes of Israel. But in Genesis 25:24–34, he and his fraternal twin brother, Esau, are not presented in the best light. After a hunting expedition, Esau comes home famished and asks Jacob for some stew. Jacob first asks him to sell him his birthright. Esau, showing very little foresight indeed, does just that. Esau is not the sharpest knife in the drawer, but Jacob *takes advantage* of his brother. Then in chapter 27 we read of Jacob's scheme, hatched by his mother Rebekah, to trick the nearly blind Isaac into giving him the blessing rightfully reserved for Esau as firstborn. Jacob, Israel's ancestor, is a liar; his exploits are hardly the stuff of character building.

There is no more central Old Testament figure than Moses. God accomplishes great things through him: the Israelites are released from Egyptian slavery, the law is given, the tabernacle is built, and the chosen people reach the edge of the Promised Land. These are some pretty big and important steps. But the Israelites didn't get this far because of Moses' character. Moses' behavior illustrates, once again, that the focus of the stories about him is actually *God's faithfulness* in redeeming his people. Everything that God did was designed to keep the promise God made to Abraham (Exodus 2:24–25). Moses was his instrument, shaped by God from birth.

If we focus on Moses' behavior instead, we see the same sort of moral mix we saw with Abraham. In Exodus 2 we see Moses, in a sneaky and impetuous manner, killing an Egyptian and hiding his body in the sand. A few verses later, he flees into the desert and makes his way to Midian. This is anything but a statement of his fine character.

In fact, the focus of this part of the story is hardly on Moses at all, as a person, but on Moses as representative of what will later happen to Israel. Israel, too, will leave Egypt and flee to Midian. As Israel's leader, *Moses acts in ways that anticipate Israel's later experiences*. This is the point the text is making, not "watch Moses and be or not be like him." There is a richness here that a character study could miss.

Moses was far from a model of virtue. Sure, he had his high points, but studying these high points *is not the reason why the story of Moses was written*. If we limit our reading of the Moses story to deriving life lessons from his actions, we diminish the power of the story as a whole. The story, once again, tells us more about God than anything. And from a Christian point of view, as Hebrews 3:1–6 makes clear, Moses is ultimately a preview of Christ. Just as Moses led his people out of slavery and into God's presence, Jesus is the new and improved Moses who leads his people out of slavery to sin and into the heavenly Promised Land. If we understand the story of Moses as part of a bigger story—a story that is about *God* rather than Moses—the full picture given in the New Testament will take on deeper meaning.

Finally, let's look at David. David is the poster child for all sorts of modern causes: leadership in business and in the church, overcoming large obstacles, etc. But like the others, David's story is part of a larger story about God. Yes, David was a great king, even if he was imperfect. But *his* kingship is not the central point of the narrative.

David was a faithful friend to Jonathan, Saul's son. And when he had the chance to kill Saul, who really seemed to deserve it, David would have none of it. He had integrity and humility. Earlier, when he fought Goliath, it certainly took courage—a kid against a giant. But we should not forget David's failings. The most notable one is his adultery with Bathsheba, which included sending her husband, Uriah, on a frontline suicide mission. David paid for that with the death of his son, and he repented (see Psalm 51). As we read in 2 Samuel 24, David sins by taking a count of his fighting men, and Israel falls under a plague as a result.

Many sermons are preached with a theme that sounds something like "be like David" (or perhaps more commonly "dare to be a Daniel" who stands fast in the "lion's den"). Again, this is not *why* these stories are in the Bible.

Kings in Israel acted as God's representatives. They also presented a snapshot of where God's plan was headed: one day the King of kings will come, one who truly represents God, who himself is the image of God, whose life will be without sin and who will lead his people in obedience. Think of the Goliath episode. So often we hear of little David standing up to the bully giant Goliath; he is cunning and faithful, with wonderful results. But the point of this story is not "have courage like David." Rather, this story points to two grander ideas.

First, the focus here is not on David the person, but on David as one who will *embody the office of king*. What does he do? He trusts God fully, obeys him, and is not at all daunted by overwhelming odds. The purpose of the story is not to model behavior for *us* but to point us to what a *true king of Israel* should look like.

Second, David's kingship is a true but imperfect "first run through" of Jesus' kingship to come. When you read the David and Goliath story, resist the temptation to see yourself in David's role. Rather, see Jesus. David does not represent us, facing down challenges at work or school; David represents Jesus—David's heir— doing the fight *for us*. If you want to see yourself in the story, you are among the people on the hillside, cheering him on. David's victory over Goliath is not only *his* victory; it is a victory for *all* the people. In the same way, Jesus has defeated the enemy, sin and death, for us. We are swept up in our King's victory, as were the Israelites under David.

Character studies sell the Bible short. They do not reflect the reasons why the stories were recorded in the first place, and they do not reflect the bigger picture: how Jesus fulfills the purposes of these Old Testament characters. Doing character studies is like playing in a puddle when you could be swimming in the ocean. Both will get you wet, but the ocean is a whole lot more interesting.

Not a "Book-by-Book" Approach

Reading the Bible book by book is an extremely important thing to do. Entire books of the Bible, not just individual verses, form our thinking.

But we are dealing with young people. Book studies, as important as they are, typically require an adult attention span. To be fruitful, book studies also require a certain base knowledge. To go back to the analogy I used at the very beginning, the more hooks and shelves you have in your closet, the more the details can be organized in a way that makes sense.

The focus in the approach I outline (as you will see in Part Two) is not on a study of each book *in detail*, but on the flow of the story *in general*. This overview of the biblical *drama* will help make subsequent book studies by your children in their adult years more profitable.

Adults can and should study the Bible in books—or at least in large chunks. But this is too much for many young students, and particularly for very young children—so the tendency has been to move to Bible stories or character studies instead. But there is a better way: get to know Jesus, then see the broad brush strokes of the biblical story, and then begin looking at the Bible in a more adult fashion in the high-school years by addressing some of the bigger issues.

Not a "Defensive" Approach

Most of us are familiar with the controversies surrounding Genesis and science. Battles have raged, most famously in the Scopes trial of the 1920s, and more recently in the Intelligent Design debate (such as the case in Dover, Pennsylvania, that made national headlines in 2005).

These debates have come about because Christians have attempted to apply the Bible to current events and current discoveries that the Bible does not speak to. Expecting from the Bible things it may not be prepared to deliver can encourage a defensive, even argumentative, approach. Sometimes defending the Bible (with humility) is important and necessary. The difficulty comes when we *teach the Bible* in such a way that we *focus* on the conflicts, rather than on laying the groundwork for a lifetime of study.

The Bible is not a book that was written to be defended. Yes, defending the Bible and Christianity has its place. But just because you can defend the Bible doesn't mean that you understand it. You can argue about whether or not the Exodus is a historical event—but that won't help you understand the book of Exodus.

A defense of Scripture is only as good as what lies beneath it, which should be a mature understanding of the nature of the Bible. Too often, I see Christians defending positions that are based on a false understanding of the biblical story. These positions may temporarily convince young children of the Bible's truth, but as children begin to think for themselves, free of their parents' protection, the inadequacy of the arguments they have been taught may become clear.

As we teach the Bible to our children, we should not be *focused* on defending a particular view of Genesis—or on any other controversial issue. There will be time for this later. Rather, the biblical story should be presented in a positive manner, keeping a focus on the bigger portrait the Bible is painting. We must learn to let the Bible have its way with us, learn to ask *its* questions first, rather than rush to it with ours.

Many of the details of the biblical story may seem strange to us (and even downright weird). But the story as a whole is one of a good and wise God doing unexpected things for an undeserving yet chosen people. This culminates in a vivid description of a new world that begins with Jesus' resurrection. In this new world, death is conquered and we can begin to live as we were created to live.

This is the picture we want our children to see. This is the image we want them to carry with them throughout their lives, for good times and for bad.

The Bible is a book that is meant to be on the "offensive," aggressively presenting a God who goes to great lengths to put the world back as it should be. If there is any "defensiveness" in our teaching of Scripture, it should come during the high-school years. At that point, it is appropriate to discuss challenges to Scripture, what they imply, and how they should be addressed constructively. But remember that a proper defense is only as good as one's *mature* understanding of what one is defending. Learning the biblical story *first* allows our children to have a mature grasp of the issues, rather than falling victim to fear, exaggeration, or a false sense of security.

I have seen many times, as I am sure you have, young people walking away from the faith because they see it as irrelevant. The first two parts of the pattern I suggest are aimed at keeping that from happening. When the really hard questions about the Bible and the Christian faith hit home during the high-school years, you can *build* on the foundation of the previous years.

What we should avoid, at all costs, is presenting difficult issues at early ages, giving simplistic answers, and then wondering why, at the age of fifteen or so, our children walk away from a faith that they find childish.

— Chapter Five —

A Final Word

As parents, we should always be thinking of what our children will look like in the future: as they approach adolescence, during their young adulthood, when they are grown, and when they reach other challenging stages in their lives.

As I write this I am in my late forties. Like most men, I have been experiencing over the last several years a condition often known as "midlife crisis." It's real, trust me. Many times I have said to myself, "I wish I had been better, more deliberately, prepared by my parents and the church for the challenges I am experiencing now."

Your child will only be under your direct teaching for a very short time. As parents of grown children can universally attest, children turn eighteen before you know it and then they are out of the house—out from under your close supervision.

Think ahead.

Realize that all that we do, including teaching our children about our faith, is ultimately geared toward helping them be *adults*. This encompasses *much more* than learning about what is in the

Bible. It involves learning what it means to be a faithful follower of Jesus in a world that is not supportive of that goal.

How we teach the Bible to our children will—I am convinced—have an effect on how they are able to handle life self-consciously as Christians. But we cannot predict the future; our only responsibility is to do the very best we can here and now.

For literally thousands of years, parents have accepted the challenge of teaching their children what they believe and why. We see echoes of this at least as far back as the Passover, where children ask their parents, "What is the significance of this ritual?" (see Exodus 12:26–27). Deuteronomy 6:4–7, one of the more memorable verses in the Pentateuch, is quite clear about the duty of Israelite parents to rehearse the Law with their children, whether they are sitting, walking, or lying down. The book of Proverbs is really an extended teaching moment, where the father and mother say, "Listen, my son" (see Proverbs 1:8). In the New Testament, Paul commends young Timothy for the faith that is in him that was first in his grandmother and mother (2 Timothy 1:5).

This responsibility is one that Jewish and Christian parents have followed with sincerity, gravity, and diligence for 2,000 years and more. When we today take on the same task, we step into a wonderful, time-honored tradition.

Remember that you are not the first parents to face this challenge—and you are not the first parents to have misgivings and anxieties about it. Many, many have gone before you, and you are now part of this brotherhood and sisterhood.

That is an honor and a reason to rejoice.

PART TWO

Reading the Story for Yourself: The Five Acts of the Bible

An introduction to the narrative pattern of the Bible

— Chapter Six —

Creation and Fall

Genesis 1–11: Creation and Fall

Not to worry, here. We are not going to go through every book of the Bible in detail. Remember my daughter's room? Now it's time to put up a few hooks and shelves to *begin* bringing some organization to our minds as we turn to the Bible itself.

The Bible is basically a story with a three-part structure. The first part of the story is creation (that only takes two chapters, Genesis 1–2). In the second part of the story, something goes very wrong (Genesis 3–11). The third part of the story is what God does through Israel to set everything right. That is the rest of the Bible, or 1,178 chapters for those of you counting.

You will most often see this three-part structure referred to as Creation, Fall, and Redemption. This is the basic plotline Christians have been working with for many, many centuries; I will adopt it too, but with some modification.

The simplicity of this three-part structure shouldn't fool us. Clearly there's a lot going on in the third part of the story—1,178 chapters worth. We can't simply call that whole part "Redemption" and think that we've understood it.

Much of what we will be looking at below is how this redemption idea is fleshed out from Genesis 12 through Revelation 22. The redemption part of the story has a *lot* of important developments (Jesus being the central one), a few twists and turns, and a couple of unexpected movements.

But it all ends well.

• • •

What is the Bible saying to us in Genesis 1–11? What are we supposed to understand about God's work in the world from these chapters?

We know that Genesis 1 bears some pretty striking similarities to creation stories of other nations of the ancient world; this is something scholars have been addressing since the mid-nineteenth century at least. There are some powerful implications of this. First and foremost, Genesis 1 is making a strong theological statement: Israel's God, unlike the gods of the other nations, created the world alone, by his word/will, and this shows the Israelites that their God alone is worthy of Israel's worship.

Right from the very beginning, the Bible is making a point about who God is and how his people are supposed to respond. Remember, Israel was surrounded by other nations, all of whom worshiped numerous gods. And if you remember your Old Testament, one of the recurring temptations for Israel was to worship these gods, whether in Egypt (in slavery), Canaan (in their own land), or Babylon (while in exile). But Genesis 1 makes the bold—*very* bold—statement that this God of desert dwellers and slaves *alone* made everything that is. This God—of whom Egypt's king said "I don't know who this god of yours even *is*" (see Exodus 5:2)—is *the* Creator.

This statement is all the more striking when you realize that the creation stories of the other nations usually involved conflict among the gods, with conflict leading to the creation. In the Babylonian creation story known to us as *Enuma Elish*, the sky and earth are created after a battle where one god kills another and cuts her in half.

Genesis 1 is a strong argument *against* such stories as these. The intent of the creation account is to keep Israel from falling into the trap of worshiping someone other than the *true* Creator. This is both repeated and developed further in the rest of the Old Testament. Continually, the reasons given for why Yahweh[4] should be worshiped are that he is not only (1) the Creator, but also (2) the deliverer (first from Egypt, then from Babylon). This dual theme continues into the New Testament: the Creator is the Redeemer.

The second important theological lesson taught by Genesis 1 is this: the creation story is about God making *order out of chaos*. When Genesis 1 describes God creating, it shows God putting everything in its place.

A key phrase is found in verse 2: "formless and void." The Hebrew term is *tohubohu*, which, believe it or not, has actually found its way into English dictionaries. It means something utterly chaotic. (I am thinking of making up a plaque and hanging it on the door of a certain child.) *Tohu* means "formless" and *bohu* means "void." When we look at the six days of creation in Genesis 1, we can see that in the first three days, God provides form to what is

---

[4]Israel's God is known by a variety of names in the Old Testament, but the two most common are God (the Hebrew word is *Elohim*) and Yahweh. The name Yahweh is worth a closer look. The Hebrew word is made up of only four consonants, YHWH (which is why it is called the tetragrammaton, Greek for "four letters"). No one actually knows how the name was pronounced, but the vowels /a/ and /e/ are added for convenience. In most English translations, the name is translated LORD (note the small capital letters). I guess this will have to do, but "LORD" obscures the fact that "Yahweh" is a *name* by which Israel's God was known as distinct from all the other named gods of the ancient world. This is why I prefer to use the name "Yahweh" throughout (unless quoting an English version), although I will also refer to Israel's God as "God."

formless; the next three days, he fills the voids. In the chart below, note how day 1 corresponds to day 4, day 2 to day 5, and day 3 to day 6.

Form out of Formlessness	Filling the Void
Day 1 light and darkness separated	Day 4 sun, moon, stars
Day 2 dome to separate the waters	Day 5 sea creatures and birds (also vegetation)
Day 3 land and sea separated	Day 6 land creatures and humanity
	Day 7 Rest	

So in Genesis 1, God straightens things up (form) in days 1–3, and then makes things to fill those spaces (void) in days 4–6. And everything is good, especially human beings. That is why the sixth day is deemed "*very* good."

This notion of "order out of chaos" is extremely important for understanding the Old Testament story. God is setting boundaries: the sea goes here, the land goes there; birds live here, crawling things live there. But the biggest boundary is between God and humans.

This is the third lesson to be learned from Genesis 1. God made humanity not simply "good" (without sin), but the crowning achievement of his creative work. Of all God's creation, only humanity is made in the image and likeness of God to rule over everything (Genesis 1:26).

This is too important to pass by quickly: humanity is special to God. In other ancient creation stories, we see gods fighting the forces of chaos and taming them. But in those stories, humans are created to do the work the gods don't want to do, or to serve the gods as slaves, or just because the gods got bored. In the Bible, humans are God's earthly *representatives*.

It is not exaggerating the message of Genesis 1 to say that humans, in their role of leadership over creation, are god-like beings on earth. This is another theme that recurs in the Bible, and especially in the New Testament. Think for a moment of Jesus, the *Son of God*, who said things such as "if you have seen me, you have seen the Father" (John 14:9), and whom Paul calls the "last Adam" (I Corinthians 15:45) after the "pattern" of the first Adam (Romans 5:14). Jesus is what Adam was supposed to have been: God's perfect representative on earth.

This brings us to what is typically called "the Fall" (Genesis 3). The story is one of doubting what God says and acting contrary to it. There is a serpent of some sort (who apparently began with legs; Genesis 3:14), a temptation that centers on whether or not God is keeping something good from the first humans, and an unidentified piece of fruit from the tree of the knowledge of good and evil. The punishment for acting contrary to God's words is swift and includes Eve's pain in childbirth, the struggle of daily work, and most important, the banishment of Adam and Eve from the Garden.

But there is more to this story than we sometimes appreciate. In the Fall, something very important was lost, and the rest of the Bible tells the story of the lengths to which God goes to get it back. Not until Revelation 22 is the mission finally, fully accomplished.

So what was lost?

We should try to think of the Fall not simply as "God made a rule but humans disobeyed." The problem runs much deeper than that. There is nothing wrong with knowing good and evil. In fact, you might think that God would actually *want* Adam and Eve to eat of this tree. But what is at issue here is *how* the first humans decide to gain this knowledge. Rather than doing it God's way, by eating of the fruit of the tree of good and evil, the first humans took matters into their own hands and *tried to be like God* in their own way. In other words, they tried to break down the boundary God had erected, part of the order he made out of chaos.

In eating the fruit, humans became agents of chaos in disrespecting the boundary God had established. They were not simply being naughty: they were acting contrary to the creation order. Taking the fruit was like pulling at the loose end of a knitted sweater and watching the whole thing unravel. This is at the root of human woes: forgetting the place that God has made for us. We are the *height* of his *creation*. He even wants us to be like him, knowing good from evil. But it has to be done his way, through obedience to him. We are *not* the *Creator*.

Chapters 4–11 perform a number of functions, but the most central is to show the spreading effects of chapter 3. Genesis 1–11 is broad in scope, looking at the human condition in general.

The story of Cain and Abel is the story of the first crime: murder. Chaos threatens to disorder God's creation. Humanity is created in the image and likeness of God (Genesis 1:26–27), but here jealousy and murder—indeed, fratricide—come on the scene quickly. First we see the proper boundaries between God and humanity disrupted by Adam and Eve. Now the proper boundaries between humans are trampled. By the time you get to the fourth chapter of Genesis, things have devolved in a way that you could never have anticipated from Genesis 1–2.

The stories of the Flood and Tower of Babel (Genesis 6–9 and 11) show how humanity has failed to live up to its design as image-bearer of God ("every inclination of the thoughts of the human heart was only evil all the time," Genesis 6:5). The Flood should be seen as a "reversal of creation," a reintroduction of chaos, followed by a "second creation." God sees how bad things have gotten and is determined to start over with Noah and his family. So what does God do? He unleashes the waters above and below, the very waters that had been kept in their proper place in Genesis 1. He allows chaos to undo the order he has established. Humans are no longer kept safe from the chaos; instead the powers of chaos are used to kill humans, the crowning achievement of God's creation. Things are unraveling in a very unsettling way.[5]

---

[5]To glance ahead, this is not the only time we will see a "creation reversal" in the Bible. In Exodus, several of the ten plagues are further examples of God unleashing creation and crossing boundaries: frogs hopping all over the homes

Noah and his family are saved, but old habits die hard. No sooner do they get off the boat than the shenanigans begin again (see Genesis 9:18–29) and their relationships began to break down. But from this dysfunctional family the world is repopulated, which leads to the Tower of Babel story, an attempt to "reach to the heavens" (Genesis 11:4). To use the language of "order," the Tower of Babel is another attempt to obliterate the line between humanity and God.

God's creation, his order out of chaos, was still threatened by disorder. What began with Adam and Eve and the forbidden fruit has had swift and far-reaching repercussions. You might say that "chaos" has never quite been fully set in order.

The remainder of the Bible tells us what God intends to do about that.

---

of men, darkness where there was light. In the crossing of the Red Sea, sea and land are separated (as they are in creation), but when the Egyptians try to pass through, the waters held at bay come crashing down (as in the Flood). In the New Testament, Jesus is a force of new creation, as seen at the very outset of John's Gospel ("In the beginning was the Word"). As Paul says in 2 Corinthians 5, anyone in Christ is a "new creation."

— Chapter Seven —

Redemption: Abraham and Moses

Redemption, Stage One: Abraham

Genesis 1–11 has been a prelude to the heart of the biblical story: God's redemption of his people, their deliverance and rescue.

Enter Abraham in Genesis 12 (or if you want to get technical, Abram, since his name is not changed to Abraham until chapter 17). Abraham is the father of the Hebrews; from him come Isaac, Jacob (renamed Israel), and Joseph. At the beginning of the story, we find Abraham in Mesopotamia: the area around Babylon, "between the rivers" (which is what "Mesopotamia" means). Those two rivers are the Tigris and Euphrates, which can still be found on the world map today.

Abraham's pagan origin is clear; it is even mentioned in Joshua 24:1–2. It is a bit unexpected, is it not, that the first ancestor of the Israelites should be so closely associated with a part of the world that will give the Israelites so much trouble in the future? After all, the Babylonians are the ones who will take the southern kingdom captive in about 586 B.C. (see 2 Kings 25).

Yet it is from these people that Abraham was chosen, for reasons completely unexplained by the biblical story. Later, this will lead to a whole host of stories told about Abraham, among Jews in the post-biblical period, in an effort to explain what Abraham *did* to deserve such an honor. But Genesis 12 is silent.

This type of silence at crucial junctures is not at all uncommon in the Old Testament. These silences are called "gaps" in the narrative, and it is sometimes hard to know whether they are gaps only to *us* (maybe the ancient Israelites were in the know) or to the Israelites as well.

I only bring this up here because, when it comes to reading and teaching the Old Testament, a lot of the action happens "in the gaps." This is where the questions come from. "What did Abraham do to deserve such an honor?" "Where did Cain get his wife from?" "How did Cain and Abel know what sacrifice even *was* at the dawn of time?" These kinds of questions come up in children's Sunday School classes all the time, perhaps because children are not yet conditioned to "know" that they shouldn't ask them! But careful readers of the Bible have been asking these questions for a long time, even hundreds of years before Jesus, thanks to the gaps in the text.

When these questions come up as you read the biblical story with your children, consider how you can use them for teaching purposes. I have three suggestions. First, affirm and encourage your child's curiosity (God can handle it). Second, mention that these kinds of questions have been asked by believers for a long time. Third, consider with your child the possibility that these things are left unsaid because they are not, for the larger purposes of the Bible, important. There is a bigger story to be told, and your focus, should, at least for now, should be on that bigger story and not on the small details. (In other words, the Bible is not a legal document intended to cover each and every question that comes up.)

Abraham traveled with his caravan up along the two rivers and stopped in Haran. Later, he was called by God to go to Canaan. Through Abraham, God would make a people for himself:

> The LORD had said to Abram, "Go from your country, your people and your father's household to the land I will show you.
>
> "I will make you into a great nation,
>   and I will bless you;
>   I will make your name great,
>   and you will be a blessing.
>   I will bless those who bless you,
>   and whoever curses you I will curse;
>   and all peoples on earth
>   will be blessed through you."[6]

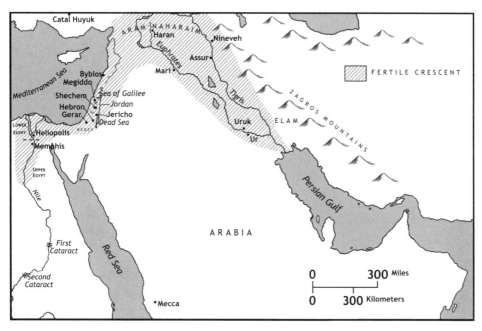

Map 1: Abraham's World

---

[6]Genesis 12:1–3

There are two things here worth highlighting, for they will come back again and again, both in the Old Testament and as a central issue in Paul's preaching of the Gospel.

First: From Abraham, God will make a nation, a *great* nation, a *blessed* nation. This nation will ultimately be called "Israel" and have "favored nation" status, so that God will bless those who bless them and curse those who curse them. You can see this theme later in Genesis and Exodus, with Egypt on the receiving end. Joseph is elevated to a place of power, and his ability to interpret dreams brings blessings to Egypt: the country is saved from famine. But later, these same Egyptians will enslave the Israelites, descendents of this same Joseph. In response, God will bring a "curse" on the Egyptians (plagues and the Red Sea incident).

Second: All the *peoples of the earth* will be blessed through this great nation. This is a very important biblical theme. God called Abraham to be the ancestor of a great nation, but not just so that a righteous law-keeping people who never get into trouble could occupy space on earth.

Keep in mind what has just happened. God's creation, which began so right, has gone all wrong. The Flood was an attempt by God to set it right, but it didn't work.[7] But now, God is taking another approach. Abraham will be the one from whom a new people will grow, a people of God's special blessing. Through them, the peoples of the world will be blessed—all those peoples not of Israel. In other words, Gentiles.

The tense relationship between Jews and Gentiles is a constant in the Bible. In the Old Testament, the Jews are commanded to be a separate people, with their own laws and their own code of

---

[7]One important side note. I know that referring to God as "attempting" something that "doesn't work" doesn't sound all that good, but that is how God is presented in this stage of the biblical story. Not every bit of mature theology is downloaded onto the opening chapters of Genesis, and it is *very* important that we allow the biblical story to be told the way *God* wants to tell it. There is a purpose to all this. The Bible is heading in a certain direction, and we need to allow the story to unfold as it does.

holiness. They are not to conform to Gentile ways. However, they are also to be a light to the Gentiles, *the means by which the nations will be reconciled to God*. As Exodus 19:6 puts it, Israel is to be a "kingdom of priests and a holy nation." Its holiness (its separateness from the nations, its "god-like-ness") is what qualifies it to be a nation of priests. And what do priests do? They *mediate* between God and humanity.

Now let's jump ahead and consider what happened to all those promises.

The task for which Israel was appointed, to be the means through which the nations were blessed, turned tragic. It was taken captive by one of those very Gentile nations it was to bless, the Babylonians. It was made an object of ridicule. In essence, the plan had failed.

This is where Jesus comes in. He completes what Israel did not. *He* becomes the means through which the nations, *both Jews and Gentiles*, will be reconciled to God ("blessed," to use the language of Genesis 12). He is the priest, the holy one, who fulfills God's righteous standards (as Israel did not). To take this one step further, according to 1 Peter 2:9, *we, the church, the people of God*, are now given that role that Jesus also has. We are a "royal priesthood and kingdom of priests." By our conduct, the nations come to understand who God is.

Quite a responsibility, isn't it? This is where the Bible is heading. We see hints of it at the very beginning of the Abraham story, which demonstrates to us that Abraham's tale is not an isolated story, the description of a great man we should emulate. Rather, Abraham stands at an initial stage in a grand story that reaches its climax, as does all of Scripture, in the death and resurrection of Christ—and, as unbelievable as it sounds, with all of us here today who are "in Christ" (as Paul so often says), who share in both his resurrection power and in his suffering (Philippians 3:10).

In a nutshell, *this* is the "moral" lesson to be learned from Scripture. This is the vision of the Christian life Scripture teaches. We are part of God's plan to restore creation.

Abraham is the man chosen to get the ball rolling, so to speak, and most of Genesis is about him and his descendents. His son Isaac is born after Sarah's childbearing years are over. Isaac marries Rebekah, after Abraham's servant travels to Abraham's homeland, Aram Naharaim, in the town of Nahor to find a wife for Isaac; Abraham intended to keep his son from marrying a Canaanite (see Genesis 24).

Rebekah gives birth to Esau and Jacob, which begins a lot of trouble.

This is a point worth stressing. Abraham is chosen as the one through whom a mighty nation will be blessed and will be a blessing to others. Yet obstacle after obstacle rises up into his way. Isaac's family is a mess; the brothers do not get along, and the mother sides with the younger boy to fool the elderly father into giving Jacob the birth*right* that *rightfully* belongs to Esau (even though he sold it for a hot meal). And never do we hear a word of rebuke from God. Instead, Jacob flees and along the way has a vision of angels ascending and descending on a ladder to heaven (ever hear of "Jacob's Ladder"?). He also gets into a wrestling match with "a man" (God), which Jacob almost wins until God puts his hip out of joint. Then Jacob's name is changed to Israel, which will become the name by which God's people will forever be known.

This is not the person I would have picked to be the father of the twelve tribes. Jacob gets a taste of his own medicine later when his father-in-law, Laban, tricks him into marrying Leah before he is able to marry Rachel, but still . . . the plan does not seem to be going smoothly.

Jacob/Israel has twelve sons (and at least one daughter), who become the twelve tribes of Israel. These tribes will be at the heart of Israel's nation status later in the Old Testament, and the Promised Land will be divided among them.

But first, we see one of the younger sons, Joseph, being ganged up against by his brothers. They are so sick of him that they fake his death, throw him into a well, and eventually sell him to traders who are on their way to Egypt. (They even make some money on the deal.) Then, they go back to an elderly Jacob, give him the bad news—they lie and tell him that Joseph was torn apart by wild beasts—and Jacob's heart almost stops beating.

Why God insists on working through these bottom-feeders is not easy to explain, but it is a constant in the Bible. God's people are marked by moral failures (David), lack of faith (Moses), and rank rebellion (most of Israel's kings). Jesus himself, although without sin, was nevertheless lowly, disgraced, and despised. And we, his people, the church, are no better.

We must think carefully about the manner in which these biblical characters are portrayed. They are morally complex—not simply "good" or "bad." This reinforces my earlier point: the central point of these stories is *not* to give us moral guidance. Certainly, we are not to walk away from the Jacob story thinking, "My, what a good lie Rebekah told. Go and do likewise." But neither is the story there simply to give a *negative* lesson about *not* lying. If it were, the Bible's main message would appear to be "If you are a good boy or girl, God will like you." The biblical drama will never be grasped as long as such a notion is allowed to predominate.

The story of Joseph sets up the Exodus from Egypt. After being sold into slavery, Joseph eventually becomes second in command to Potiphar. Joseph may be best known to many Bible readers as the man who resisted temptation, but that one incident is *not* the heart and soul of the story. Yes, Joseph did what was right, and yes, this can serve as a model for us to follow. But our question should be "How does this connect to the surrounding story, and why is it here?"

We see Joseph *grow* as a leader, from a spoiled kid to second in command in Egypt. And his lessons were learned the hard way, through suffering humiliation and injustice. The same is true of nearly every important biblical figure you can name: Abraham, Jacob, Joseph, Moses, David. They all experienced humiliation and oppression on the way to being used powerfully by God. *That* is one of the lessons to be taken from this story when it is set into the context of the surrounding narration: Don't expect an easy time of it if you are following God. This was true of Israel's leaders. It was true of Israel as a nation. It was true of Jesus himself. And it is true of all of us.

Joseph's momentary hardships chiseled him into a man of God, and God used Joseph in ways he never could have expected. Joseph saved Egypt from starvation, reunited his family, and brought them all to live with him in Egypt. But all of that was simply prelude to another story, one where God would employ yet another severe hardship in order to exalt his people and form a nation that would embody his image.

So this first stage in redemption is about God's formation of a new people, beginning with Abraham. The process is not smooth, for God's people are deeply flawed. Yet God is intent on shaping them into the kind of people who reflect his image to the world around them.

We come, then, to the Exodus and the journey to Mount Sinai, where the instructions for holy living (the Law) and holy worship (the tabernacle) are given. And the central figure here, arguably *the* most important person in all of the Old Testament, is Moses.

Redemption, Stage Two: Moses

The story of Moses and the Exodus from Egypt is the second stage in God's redemptive actions. Here, Israel is delivered from slavery and her journey as an actual *nation* begins. This is fundamentally an act of grace on God's part; he brings the Israelites out of Egypt not because they are good people or because he feels sorry for them, but because he has an important role for them to play on a grand scale.

The basic gist of the story is well known, perhaps because generations have seen Charlton Heston portray Moses in *The Ten Commandments*. The Israelites are enslaved by a no-good Pharaoh, God raises up a deliverer, ten plagues afflict Egypt, the Red Sea parts, the Israelites arrive at Mount Sinai, and the Israelites worship a golden calf instead of God.

The familiarity of the story can obscure how central this stage is in God's plan.

The story of the Exodus is a story of liberation from slavery, but there is much more to be learned from it. By the beginning of chapter 19, we have arrived at Mount Sinai, far from Egypt and liberation. The Ten Commandments are then given, but that is just the tip of the iceberg. There are pages and pages of other laws (often called the Book of the Covenant), as well as an immense amount of space devoted to the building of the tabernacle. This should give us a clue: the purpose of the Exodus was more involved than simply the freeing of slaves.

In the first place, God delivers the Israelites as part of the promise he made to Abraham (Exodus 2:24–25). The story of Abraham is *connected* to the story of the Exodus; together the two show us that God is a promise-keeping God. He delivers Israel because of his love for his people, but also because he "remembered" his covenant with Abraham, Isaac, and Jacob. With that remembrance, God is on the move to bring his project, begun in Abraham, to a new level.

In the second place, Israel is shown to belong solely to God. The Exodus story is often misunderstood only as a story of justice, showing how God hates slavery and wants his people to be free. But although social justice is a big theme in some of the Minor Prophets, it doesn't really come into view in Exodus. Moses does not say to Pharaoh, "Let my people go." He says, "Let my people go *so that they may worship me.*" There is a big difference between these two.

A little bit of Hebrew will (believe it or not) make the point clearer. The Israelites are slaves to the Egyptians; they *serve* Pharaoh. The Hebrew word for "serve" is *'avad.* It also means "worship." What we see in Exodus is a tug of war between Pharaoh, who says "Israel will *'avad* (be slaves to) me," and God who says, "No, Israel will *'avad* (worship) me." The central issue in Exodus is: Whom will Israel *'avad?* Will the Israelites *be slaves* to Pharaoh or *worship* Yahweh? Pharaoh and Yahweh are rival competitors for Israel's allegiance.

We all know who wins that battle. The plagues commence, and there is no contest. This God of slaves, this desert-dwelling God, marches onto Egyptian soil and takes on their king and their gods and makes his point: "Israel is *mine* and they will *'avad* ME!"

This is why the time at Mount Sinai is so important. Arriving at Mount Sinai is *the point* of the Exodus. Here, the Israelites first really worship Yahweh. They hear the thunder and see the lightning and smoke. They are meeting their God: their Creator and Deliverer.

Now we can see the importance of the laws of Exodus, and of those detailed descriptions of the tabernacle—two topics that take up about half of the book.

The Law was not intended just to give the Israelites rules to follow and to keep them in line. And it *certainly* was not intended to give the Israelites a way to prove themselves worthy of Yahweh through observance of each stricture. The Law was not given to people *so that* they can be redeemed. The Law was given to a people *already* redeemed. God's grace comes first—always. Because the Israelites *already are* God's people, God delivers them and gives them the Law (remember the promise to Abraham).

The Law is not the means by which the Israelites lay claim to being God's children. It is what God gives to those who already are.

I stress this point because my experience as a professor and as a parent has made it clear to me that grace is a very hard lesson to learn. Many of us are legalists at heart. I am continually amazed by how many Christians (myself included) really believe deep down, when all the surface rhetoric is stripped away, that we need to earn God's favor. But that is not the function of law, either in the Old Testament or in the New Testament. The Law is not the way to gain God's favor; it is a gift to those who already are favored.

The laws in Exodus were given to this favored people so that they would have a pattern for what it truly means to "serve" (*'avad*) God. In truth, the Israelites were not freed from "service" when God brought them out of Egypt. They were transferred from one form of "slavery" to another. God was forming them into a people who would *reflect the image of God to a fallen world*. That is the point of the Law. "When you enter Canaan, be like *this*. Don't do what they do. You are to be my *representatives*. You are to be a *blessing for the nations*."

Whereas the Law gives a pattern for holy behavior, the tabernacle gives a pattern for holy worship. God wants to be worshiped in a particular way—and that way is *not* Egyptian or Canaanite. Rather, God gives a blueprint for a structure that reflects him. He also gives instructions for priests and the making of sacrifices. From chapter 25 until the end of Exodus, we read about this blueprint (with one important interruption, which we'll get to in a second).

The tabernacle section is frustrating—repetitive, and apparently irrelevant to our morning devotions. But let's take a second look. Chapters 25–31 give the *instructions* for building the tabernacle. In these chapters, *seven times* we read, "And the LORD said to Moses." The seventh time this phrase occurs, the LORD says to Moses, "Say to the Israelites, 'You must observe my Sabbaths. This will be a sign between me and you for the generations to come, so you may know that I am the LORD, who makes you holy'" (Exodus 31:12–13). I hope this rings a bell; you should think immediately about Genesis 1, where we read six times, once on each of the six days of creation, "And God said, 'Let there be . . .'" And then, on the seventh day, God rests.

The tabernacle is not an ancient version of a revival tent. It is a mini-creation—a symbol of what God has brought about. Some scholars have likened it to a small version of the cosmos—angels are even depicted on the curtains hanging above. The tabernacle (and later the temple) is a new creation, a little patch of what things were like before the Fall. It is "heaven on earth." If God is going to descend to his people to be worshiped, an appropriate structure is needed: a design that reflects his heavenly home, a holy oasis amid a world gone bad.

Unfortunately, in chapters 32–34, the people take a break and worship a golden calf instead.

Moses takes too long on the mountain; the people get restless and demand that Aaron fashion a calf for them. This calf is an idol, which just means a man-made object representing a god of some sort. This particular calf represents Yahweh. The Israelites are not breaking the First Commandment ("You shall have no other gods before me")—they are breaking the Second ("You shall not make for yourself an idol in the form of anything in heaven above or on the earth beneath or in the waters below"). They are still worshiping Yahweh but by using an idol—in a way God did *not* prescribe, in a manner that reflects the nations around them, rather than in a way that will draw those nations away from their false hopes and toward God himself. The golden calf incident is not just a bump in the road, a lapse in Israel's obedience. It threatens to undo *the very reason* why the Israelites were delivered from Egypt.

The incident of the golden calf spans chapters 32–34. Chapters 35–40 pick up again with the tabernacle, but now the topic is building it, not planning it. What is very interesting, however, is that chapter 35 begins right where chapter 31 leaves off, with a discussion of the Sabbath. The passages about the Sabbath "frame" the golden calf episode. *It is as if we have not skipped a beat.* The matter of the golden calf has been dealt with, the tabernacle is completed, and the crisis is averted. God's plan continues.

The Exodus is a very important theological moment in the Old Testament. It comes up elsewhere (especially in the Psalms and in Isaiah) as *the* event the Israelites can look back to as evidence of how great Yahweh is. The Exodus proves that there is no god like him. This remembering of the Exodus continues on into the New Testament, where, in John 1, Jesus is said to "dwell" with his people. "Dwell" is from the Greek word meaning "to tabernacle." Jesus is the new tabernacle, the presence of God among his people on earth. He is also the new Moses delivering his people, not from slavery to Pharaoh, but from slavery to sin and death (Hebrews 3–4).

The Exodus story, in other words, has a *trajectory*. It is not a flat story we are to read in isolation from the rest of the Bible in order to derive a "lesson" from it. Rather, it is a crucial chapter in the grand story. This second stage of redemption is all about God forming a people for himself and training them to look like people who are his image-bearers. He is teaching them proper behavior (Law) and proper worship (tabernacle). In this way, Israel will be able to reflect God's light to those around them.

This will involve Israel eventually finding a more permanent home, rather than walking around in a desert. And so we enter into the third stage of redemption: Israel becomes a nation with land and royalty.

— Chapter Eight —

David and the Problem of Kingship

Redemption, Stage Three: David and Kingship

In the third stage of redemption, Israel is transformed from a desert-wandering tribe of former slaves to a people with land, kings, and eventually a temple. Ideally, this transformation would have produced stability for Israel and glory for God. Like a new church that starts up in a run-down neighborhood, Israel was supposed to be a godly influence in her new home.

Instead, we see 400 years of slow but steady decline.

First, the Israelite kingdom splits into two. One half is taken captive and shipped off to Assyria. The other half holds on for a few more generations until the Babylonians come and take them away. Land, temple, and the kingly line come to an end.

After the Exodus, Israel goes through a lengthy period of time that involves the conquest of Canaan. During this time, they are ruled by "judges." Don't think of a white wig and a gavel; these judges were wild, charismatic warrior types who protected Israel from oppressors and led them in battle.

Israel was, from a human point of view, the runt of the ancient litter. This little nation was under almost constant attack from the Canaanite peoples it was displacing. To make matters worse, Israel lived in a buffer state between Egypt to the south, Babylon to the east, and Assyria to the north. Controlling the land of Canaan meant controlling the ancient Near Eastern world.[8] This nation of former slaves who worshipped some unknown god had their hands full just defending their existence.

Despite the protection of the judges, the Israelites demanded that God give them a king "like the other nations." They wanted

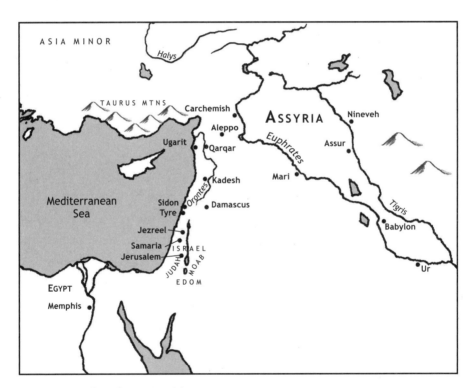

Map 2: Israel and its Neighbors

---

[8]"Ancient Near East" is the typical term used in biblical studies for the ancient Mesopotamian world of the Bible. It corresponds more or less to today's more commonly used term "Middle East."

to be like their neighbors—which for worshipers of Yahweh was contrary to God's own purposes. The Israelites were supposed to be a people who reflected *Yahweh*, not the nations around them.

Still, God approves the plan. The prophet Samuel, the last judge of Israel, is called by God to bring Israel into the next phase of its national life, when a king will rule the people. Samuel warns them that having a king will introduce a whole new set of problems—but they insist on going ahead.

God uses this kingship to bring about redemption for his people. In his hands, kingship becomes a way of realizing his purposes. The king was to lead Israel in obedience and faithfulness to God. He was to protect her from enemies, and was also to enlarge the territory of Israel in conformity with the land promises given to Abraham.

These kings were to be anointed with oil. A king was, in other words, an "anointed one." The Hebrew word for this is *mashiach* [ma-SHEE-ach]. It is from this word that we get the English word "messiah." And, incidentally, the Greek version of that word is where we get "Christ" from, so "Jesus Christ" means "Jesus the anointed one."

It is entirely accurate to understand Israel's kings as messiahs: they were anointed by God to do his work. We need to resist the temptation to think that "messiah" in the Old Testament means the supernatural, second person of the Trinity, who will die for our sins. Yes, Jesus is the ultimate and final messiah, who far exceeds anything any messiah before him did. But that is just the point. To appreciate Jesus' messianic role, how impressive and amazing it is, we need to be familiar with what the concept meant *in the Old Testament*. There, the "messianic hope" was not in a heavenly being *coming down*, but in Yahweh *raising up* a mighty warrior-king who would keep the Law and would rule and guide his people. Israel's kings were God's representatives on earth, there to rule for him as intermediaries.

Like Moses, Abraham, Noah, and Adam before them, the kings were to be the instruments through whom God's blessings to Israel and to the nations were to be funneled. Unfortunately, they don't get the job done—not even close.

The first king is Saul, a tall, good-looking guy who is a complete disaster as king. God then tells Samuel that he has someone else in mind—someone who, like Israel itself, is the runt of the litter. He is not a candidate who would make you think "king" when you saw him walking down the street. But once again, God chooses to work through the weak and unassuming.

Of course, we are talking about David. He is a good man; unlike Saul, he is humble and godly. When David slays the Philistine giant Goliath, Saul becomes jealous and testy, and even seeks permanent ways to rid himself of this problem.

But David is wise, thanks to his friend (Saul's son) Jonathan feeding him information. And David is so honorable that, even though he has chances to do away with Saul, "God's anointed," he will not. That is the stuff kings are made of.

Saul utterly fails in his task, being more concerned to further his own name than God's; David, God's choice, replaces him. And David becomes the *great* king.

True, David is not perfect. We all know about his shortcomings, the most famous of which is the Bathsheba incident. But David is repentant when he fails. He is a "man after God's own heart," as the Bible says. He becomes the model for the kings who follow him, and God promises him (via the prophet Nathan) a reign that, through his offspring, will never end.

David's reign needs to be looked at side by side with the reign of his son and successor, Solomon. Yes, Solomon takes foreign wives, a definite no-no, but he is also known for his wisdom. In the Old Testament, wisdom does not mean "being really smart." It refers to an intimacy with God that allows your life, in every sense, to reflect something of the character of God.

In David and Solomon, we see a sort of "messianic ideal." They do a good (although not perfect) job as God's earthly representatives, God's image-bearers. They are genuinely obedient and filled with love for God. It is also under David and Solomon that Israel experiences its greatest geographical expansion and develops an international reputation. Israel seems to be truly becoming a "light for the

Gentiles," a "blessing for the nations." The land promised to Abraham is in the Israelites' possession, they are at relative peace within and without, and the other nations are beginning to take notice of them.

But it doesn't last. The "messiahs" who follow David and Solomon are deeply flawed people. The corruption of the kings is the primary reason why God's chosen people are sent into exile. Everyone suffers because these representatives fail. The kingdom of Israel splits into two: the northern kingdom, made up of ten tribes, and the southern kingdom, made up of the remaining two tribes (Judah and Benjamin).

The northern kingdom is sometimes called Ephraim (the largest of the ten northern tribes), and at other times is called Israel. The southern kingdom is normally called Judah. There are nineteen kings in the north and twenty in the south. In the north, all are corrupt; they lead their people in worshiping other gods. The northern kingdom meets its end at the hands of the Assyrians, who in 722 B.C. take the ten tribes of the northern kingdom captive. This is where the notion of the "lost tribes of Israel" comes from; in fact, the tribes that went into captivity were scattered by their captors through conquered lands and were assimilated by their surroundings.

The southern kingdom fares a bit better, on two counts.

First, it holds on until about 586 B.C., when its people are taken into exile by the Babylonians. When the Persians conquer the Babylonians, *these* captives, the southerners, are allowed to return to their land; this happens in 538 B.C.

But only a "remnant" (an important biblical word) returns to the land. Only the southern tribes come back—and not every last person, either. Some stay in their new homes, having grown accustomed to their new way of life. So, the returnees are actually a remnant of a remnant. (These events are recounted in 1 and 2 Kings, plus in portions of a number of prophetic books. The temple was rebuilt in 516 B.C., and the books of Ezra and Nehemiah describe the decades that follow.)

Second, while the northern kings are almost entirely corrupt, the south has two decent rulers: Hezekiah and Josiah. The biblical writers tell us that these two kings are faithful to God and enforce proper worship (e.g., cutting down the "Asherah poles," which were common pagan worship sites).

But those two fairly good kings can't make up for the flaws and corruption of all the rest.

This is why a messianic hope springs up, especially during and after the exile. The hope is for a righteous king—a king to arise and rule with justice and righteousness, according to the law of God. Several of the prophets talk about this hope, but so do the books of 1 and 2 Chronicles.

I know, I know—boring. Chronicles starts with nine chapters of names, and then goes on to tell you about the same events you find in 1 and 2 Samuel and 1 and 2 Kings.

But don't be fooled! 1 and 2 Chronicles—really *one* book—was written after the remnant returned from Babylon: it is a *postexilic* book. And after the exile, God's people wanted a messiah—and not a flawed one like the kings that led Israel and Judah into disaster.

Of all the Old Testament books, 1 and 2 Chronicles is among the most "messianic" as we defined the word earlier. Chronicles is very concerned to see a new king arise, one like David, who will lead the people well. This king, this messiah, will be faithful in leading the people in obedience to God, and he will also protect and expand Israel's borders.

This is the Old Testament messianic hope.

When Jesus comes, not as a king but as a carpenter, he *defies* conventional messianic expectations. Then he fulfills them, in ways that go far *beyond* those expectations. This is why many of his followers—Peter especially—had such a hard time understanding his mission. For Peter, "messiah" meant a king who would get rid of the Romans so that Israel could go back to ruling itself. As far as Peter and his contemporaries were concerned, as long as a foreign power was in Israel and was in charge, Israel could not truly be Israel.[9]

---

[9] See Matthew 16:21–25.

But Jesus had other plans. First, he would have to purify Jew and Gentile alike, to be a "blessing" to all peoples (think of Abraham here). That was stage one. Stage two began at his resurrection and continues to his second coming. Jesus was crowned king—not just over a small plot of land in the ancient Near East, but over the entire world (look at Matthew 28:16–20).

Jesus redefined the messianic role. At the same time, the New Testament makes his connection to David very clear. Jesus is descended from David by blood, through Mary. And in Christ, the Davidic ideal is finally and properly fulfilled. As God's divine representative to all peoples, Jew and Gentile, Jesus does what no forerunner had been able to do—reverse the damage caused by the first human, the first representative of God on earth, the first image-bearer: Adam.

The Davidic stage of redemption helps set the stage for Jesus and his fulfillment of this kingly/messianic role, centuries later. Jesus would be truly faithful in leading his people. He would show his people what it means to know God and to be known by him. He would fulfill the kingly ideal. But he would do so in ways that no one expected.

— Chapter Nine —

The Return from Babylon

Redemption, Stage Four: Return from Babylon

By the end of the third stage of redemption, Israel is just return-ing from its tragic captivity in Babylon, the great superpower of the time. In the fourth stage of redemption, God brings his people back and reestablishes them in the land.

Let's go back to that third stage for just a minute. Remember, the southern kingdom, Judah, was made up of two of the twelve tribes: Judah and Benjamin. The Judahites lasted about 130 years longer than the Ephraimites (the people of the northern kingdom), who were taken captive by the Assyrians in 722 B.C.

In both kingdoms, the failure of the kings to uphold Yahweh's standards of kingship led to the exile. We see that standard laid out in such places as Deuteronomy 17:14–20, where, among other things, kings are to "follow carefully all . . . of this law and these decrees" (v. 19). If they do so, they and their descendents "will reign a long time over his kingdom in Israel" (v. 20).

That didn't happen; instead the kings were corrupt. Before the exile, we see the prophet Habakkuk[10] complaining to God about the corruption of the leaders. The conversation goes something like this:

Habakkuk: Lord, there is corruption everywhere. Won't you do something about it?

The Lord: I will.

Habakkuk: Great! What do you have in mind (perhaps a plague of some sort)?

The Lord: Oh, I'll tell you, but you won't believe it, even when you hear it.

Habakkuk: (This sounds bad).

The Lord: I am going to send the Babylonians, your enemies, to invade and teach everyone a lesson.

Habakkuk: That's not exactly what I had in mind.

The Babylonian invasion and exile was God's idea.

But the captivity is only for a time. It serves a purpose: to refine God's people, as by fire, and to bring a faithful remnant back to the land. With this people, God will, once again, start over.

Judah's return to the land (we can go ahead and call this remnant "Israel" again, since it is all that's left of the twelve tribes) is a new beginning. God is "re-creating" Israel.

Israel *suffered* in her exile: the Israelites were away from the land promised to them by God; they had no temple in which to worship him. They were utterly despised and rejected. But through this suffering the Israelites were purged and purified, fit for the task of beginning anew.

Israel's exile, rejection, and suffering in Babylon foreshadow Jesus' own rejection and suffering on behalf of his people. The famous prophecy in Isaiah 53 about the "suffering servant" is primarily referring to the suffering of *Israel*, God's servant. It is *ultimately* fulfilled in Jesus and his suffering for his people. But God is not finished with Israel yet.

---

[10]*Everyone* misspells this name, even scholars from time to time. Impress your friends: it is one *b* and three *k*s (not two *b*s and two *k*s).

And so we read the famous words of Isaiah 40:1–5:

> Comfort, comfort my people, says your God.
> Speak tenderly to Jerusalem,
> and proclaim to her
> that her hard service has been completed,
> that her sin has been paid for,
> that she has received from the LORD's hand
> double for all her sins.
> A voice of one calling:
> "In the wilderness prepare
> the way for the LORD;
> Make straight in the desert
> A highway for our God.
> Every valley shall be raised up,
> every mountain and hill made low;
> the rough ground shall become level,
> the rugged places a plain.
> And the glory of the LORD will be revealed,
> and all people will see it together.
> For the mouth of the LORD has spoken."

These words refer to Israel's return from Babylon (which is the main topic of Isaiah, beginning at chapter 40). Here, the people are to be comforted and spoken to tenderly. They are told that the tough times are over, that their sin has been paid for, and they are about to receive "double" for all their sins (meaning that the new situation will be twice as good as the hardship was bad).

And here is how the Lord is going to do it: He is coming to Babylon. A way is to be prepared for him in the wilderness, a highway in the desert.

This is significant. The way to get back and forth from Canaan and Babylon was to travel via the Fertile Crescent as Abraham had done, where water is plentiful, not through the desert (see p. 69).

But Yahweh will take the short cut. This is why the wilderness/desert will be made straight, the low places raised up, and the high places leveled out. A smooth road is being paved, because God is coming and he is in a hurry. And his "glory" will be revealed—meaning that all will see him delivering his people from captivity.

And so, Israel returns to its land.

The Persians, mentioned earlier, had a policy of allowing captives to return home with relative freedom, so long as they didn't cause trouble. Israel could now worship Yahweh properly—which meant the rebuilding of the temple.

The temple was completed in 516 B.C., a shell of its former self. The Israelites were back in the land, but they were still subject to a foreign power.

The Persian dynasty lasted a long time, well into the fourth century B.C. During this period, Aramaic, the international language of the day, came to replace Hebrew as the common language for the Jews. So that all Jews could read the Hebrew Bible, it began to be translated into Aramaic.

This is an extremely important point: *Israel was going international*. Now, other peoples could have access to the Bible in their own language.

In 330 B.C., the Greek warrior-king Alexander the Great took over the known world. And so, after a time, Greek became the language of choice. In the centuries to follow, a mixture of languages was spoken in the land of Israel. Hebrew was still in use, but mainly by Jewish leaders. Aramaic was alive and well, and so was Greek. Then, with the Roman takeover of the known world, Latin entered the mix. According to John 19:20, the sign hung over Jesus' cross ("Jesus of Nazareth King of the Jews")[11] was written in Aramaic, Greek, and Latin.

---

[11]This sign is also known to Christians as INRI, which is an acronym for "Jesus of Nazareth, King of the Jews" in Latin. Jesus is spelled with an "I," "R" is for the Latin word for king, "rex," and the second "I" is the first letter in the Latin spelling for "Jew." For those of you who *really* have nothing else to think about, the Greek versions of "Jesus" and "Jew" also begin with the Greek letter "I." Jesus's name in Greek is *Iesous* (ee-ay-SOOS). The "J" is a later, European development.

Thanks to the Greek takeover, the Hebrew Bible—what we now call the Old Testament—was translated after a time into Greek as well as Aramaic. The Greek Old Testament became known as the "Septuagint" because, according to tradition, it was completed in seventy days. (The root "sept" means seven, and the common abbreviation for this translation is the Roman numeral LXX, seventy).

By the time Jesus came on the scene, the world was already speaking Greek, and this is the language that the New Testament was written in. When the Gospel began to spread, it spread in Greek to a people who were already prepared, at least linguistically, to hear it. Just as Jesus became one of us, the Bible took on the language that people were actually speaking.

So Israel's return from Babylon put the Israelites back into their land, but it introduced a mixture of peoples, languages, and customs into the land as well. This made the land of Israel volatile, especially during Jesus' time on earth. First-century Palestine was a very tense place.

Into this situation, Jesus came. I have heard it put this way: If you knew nothing of Jesus or Christianity, but you understood the tense political, cultural, and religious mood of the first century, and then you started reading the Gospels, it wouldn't be long before you asked yourself "Who is this Jesus and when is he going to be killed?"

The fifth act of redemption is the final act. It begins with Jesus' arrival in the powder keg of Palestine; and it is all about the Gospel, the climax of redemption, the final push "back to the Garden."

Chapter Ten

Jesus: Scene One and Scene Two

Redemption, Stage Five: Jesus (Scene One)

Jesus' coming to earth begins the fifth and final act of God's redemption, but it occurs in two stages. The first stage is his first coming, the second stage is his second coming.

There is disagreement among some Christians about the second stage—namely about whether there will be a period of Christ's reign on earth before the real end. But we don't need to rehash those debates in order to understand what that second stage is *about*.

Let's start with Jesus' *first* coming, which is the focus of the Gospels and much of the material in the Epistles. Jesus came to reveal to his people God in his fullness. He was God's son—which means that he, like David and the other kings of Israel, and like Adam before them, was God's earthly representative.

The twist, of course, is that Jesus' sonship has a more direct connection to God—a "genetic connection" to the Father. He is more than an image-bearer of God. It is a mystery, but to see Jesus *is* to see the Father, for he and the Father are one. Jesus, in other words, is divine.

Still, as Paul puts it in Philippians 2:6–8, Jesus did not consider equality with God something to be held on to, and so he willingly became a man—a man born in low circumstances, persistently misunderstood and mocked. Jesus lived his life in a state of double humiliation: he was God become man, and as a man he was nothing much to look at.

Once again God chooses to show his glory through the humble things. God could have made himself known fully, climactically, in a good old blast of lightning, or the sky opening up. But he didn't. Jesus came as a lowly carpenter's son.

But his mission was nothing less than beginning the final stage of redemption. He was the messiah, as we discussed earlier, but not one who came from a ruling royal family and intended to wipe out the Roman invaders. His messiahship was far more sweeping. In his plan, Jews and Gentiles would *together* be made whole, forgiven of their sins, through Jesus' own death and resurrection.

Let's use some Old Testament language here that we've used in the previous four stages. Jesus came to do what no one from Adam on, including Israel as a nation, was able to do: be a blessing to all the nations, Jew and Gentile. He did this through his death and resurrection. By his death he restored humanity to God, and by his resurrection he raised all of God's people to a new life. In that new life, being an image-bearer of God is no longer a distant possibility but a present reality. Through Jesus' new people, called the church, God will continue to reconcile the world to himself.

I fear that too often we sell the biblical story short by reducing it to "Jesus died on the cross so I wouldn't go to hell." Fair enough, but this way of putting it cheapens the Gospel to *simply* a matter of "how you get saved." The Gospel certainly includes this, but there is much more to it as well. Jesus actually fulfills Israel's story thus far. Through Jesus, all the nations are truly and finally blessed, as promised through Abraham. Jesus is the new and improved Moses, who leads his people out of a different kind of slavery (sin and death) and delivers them safely to their new home. Like David, Jesus is anointed by God to lead his people. And when God delivers his people from Babylon, this is a foreshadowing in the Old Testament storyline of the time when God will bring his people home. But this home is not a piece of property along the Mediterranean Sea, but a heavenly abode, a new Garden, as we see in Revelation 22.

Jesus died and was raised to life to allow all of us to be a part of Israel's grand story. His resurrection was not just a last-minute trick God pulled off to show people his strength. Jesus' resurrection was the first part of that final, climactic stage. It was a present down payment (or to use Paul's language, a "deposit"—see 2 Corinthians 1:22 and 5:5) of what will happen more fully, more finally, at the second act of his redemption—the second coming.

Redemption, Stage Five: Jesus (Scene Two)

By being raised from the dead, Jesus became the "firstfruit" of the future resurrection of all believers (as Paul liked to put it). In other words, what happened to Jesus in his resurrection is a *preview* of what will happen to all those who are "in Christ" (another favorite phrase from Paul).

When Jesus rose from the dead, the future invaded the present. We have a real, concrete preview of what will happen to all believers, all those who are "in Christ" at the second coming.

Christians live "between the times." We live in a time where the "last days" have already begun by virtue of Jesus' resurrection, but where the final installment of the last days is in the future. In the meantime, however, what defines us as God's people is being united to God in Christ by faith. When all the church attendance books have been lost in a pile of rubble, when all our efforts to teach our children the Bible come to an end, the question remaining will be whether we are united, with Christ, to God.

This is the end of our entire study of Scripture: to help our children see the utter simplicity of the Gospel. Our understanding of Scripture should be guided by this simple vision.

To return to my very first analogy, it's like I went back into that messy child's room and said, "O.K., let's make this simple. ALL *clothes* off the floor. That's it. All of our closet organization and all of our hooks and pegs are intended to help you with that single clear objective."

The simple center of the Gospel message is often lost on adults, and therefore lost on our children too. Jesus' resurrection brought the future into the present. Because we are united with Christ, we *already* have that future built into us. And our union with Christ is so strong that our lives reflect Jesus'. Whatever happened to Jesus happens to us. Jesus died; we also died to sin and death in our baptism. Jesus was raised from the dead; so also when we are reborn in Christ we, too, are raised from death to life. Jesus ascended into heaven; so we too, as Christians, are seated *now* in the "heavenly places" (as Paul puts it).

That is an amazing concept. Although we live here and now on this earth, we are so much a part of Christ that Paul can speak of us now in future terms: being seated in heavenly places is *already happening*. We are living here and now, but the New Testament reminds us, constantly, of our union with Christ and what that has already accomplished for us.

The message of the New Testament is not "do good or God will get mad at you" (a signal that children too often pick up). Rather, the message of the New Testament is this: "You are 'in Christ' people, and that means you already have one foot in the future. You have a high calling. The power of the Spirit of Christ is at work in you, teaching you, loving you, rebuking you, carrying you if need be, so that in every area of life you can be more like Jesus. You are called from darkness into light to be true image-bearers of God. Therefore, by God's mercy, stop living in such a way that is opposite to that high calling." The message is not, "Be good, little boys and girls, or God will get you," but rather, "How can you even *think* of doing the kinds of things you used to do?" The message is not, "Do these things so that God will be pleased with you," but instead, "God *has* made you brothers and sisters with Christ; he *is* pleased with you, now *go and live it.*"

As Christians we must continually remind ourselves that our behavior stems from who we are in Christ. What we are to do in any given situation as followers of Christ is based on who we are ("in Christ" beings).

We are human beings living here and now, but by virtue of our union with the risen Christ, we have a foretaste of the future in our hearts. Our greatest task in teaching the Bible to our children is to bring them to the point where they join us "in Christ." And this is what the Bible is here to do: to tell, ultimately, the one big story of who God is and what he does to restore his world.

INDEX

See also Jesus

Resurrection of Jesus, 34, 53, 71, 87, 96–98

Scripture
compared to other texts, 40
historical context, 39–41
languages, original, 92–93
purpose of, 13, 31
See also Bible, Teaching the Bible
Septuagint, 93
Sermon on the Mount, 46
Settings (of the Bible), 38–42
Solomon, 84–85
See also David

Tabernacle, 37–38, 49, 74, 75, 76, 77–79
Teaching (the Bible)
as a whole, 7

as God's story, 29–42
Bible's similarities with Jesus, 19–22
difficulties, 9–14
summary, 55–56
Telling God's Story (curriculum), 7–8, 46n3, 29–42
Temple, 77, 81, 85, 90, 92
Ten Commandments, 10
Traditional approaches to teaching the Bible
"Bible story," 44–46
"book-by-book," 52
"character study," 47–51
"defensive," 52–54
"owner's manual," 13, 23

Wisdom, 23–27